The Reluctant Architecture of European Power

Sebastiano Fabbrini

The Reluctant Architecture of European Power

Birkhäuser
Basel

On behalf of the publisher
Acquisitions Editor: Pablo Schneider
Content Editor: Bettina R. Algieri
Production: Heike Strempel-Bevacqua

Typesetting: Savage Types Media GbR, Berlin
Image editing: Savage Types Media GbR, Berlin
Printing: Beltz Grafische Betriebe GmbH, Bad Langensalza
Paper: Magno Volume 115 g/m²
Typeface: De Gruyter Serif

MIX
Papier | Fördert gute Waldnutzung
FSC® C089473

Cover illustration: Aerial view of the EP Headquarters in Brussels. Photographer: Simon Schmitt
© European Union 2016

Library of Congress Control Number: 2025934452

Bibliographic information published by the German National Library
The German National Library lists this publication in the Deutsche Nationalbibliografie; detailed bibliographic data are available on the Internet at http://dnb.dnb.de.

ISBN 978-3-0356-2984-2
e-ISBN (PDF) 978-3-0356-2985-9

Im Westfeld 8, 4055 Basel, Switzerland
Part of Walter de Gruyter GmbH, Berlin/Boston

www.birkhauser.com
Questions about General Product Safety Regulation: productsafety@degruyterbrill.com

9 8 7 6 5 4 3 2 1

Book's Abstract

The book focuses on the European Union and its architectural productions. The hypothesis revolves around the concept of reluctance, a term that challenges the common understanding of the relationship between architecture and power. That type of reading assumes that architecture is a sophisticated political instrument and, more importantly, that every structure of power is naturally eager to use it. Countless studies have shown the varying ways in which architecture helped represent or facilitate all kinds of power dynamics throughout history. The book, on the contrary, deals with a very powerful organization that, over decades, has proven to be reluctant to use architecture in any shape or form. And it also addresses the limitations of architecture when faced with political opportunities in this arena. Analyzing several relevant cases, a simple question keeps coming up: why is it so difficult for the institutions of the European Union to engage with architecture? This book sheds light on the forces behind this short-circuit, as well as the strategies that made specific architectural productions possible under these adverse conditions.

Book's Author

Sebastiano Fabbrini (Trento, 10 November 1989 — 16 June 2024), was Assistant Professor in History of Architecture at IUAV (University Institute of Architecture in Venice). He achieved the Italian national scientific qualification (ASN) as Associate Professor in architectural history. At the IUAV, he directed the Jean Monnet module *Project Ventotene: Architecture and Power*, funded by the European Commission, and the research project *The Architecture of European Integration*, for which he was awarded the "Seal of Excellence" of the Marie Curie program and a "Young Researcher" grant of the Italian National Recovery and Resilience Plan (PNRR). Concurrently, he was visiting fellow at the Technische Universität Darmstadt (TU Darmstadt), thanks to a scholarship of the *Deutscher Akademischer Austauschdienst* (DAAD). This book stems from these research efforts, conducted over the past five years. Prior to joining IUAV, Sebastiano received his PhD in architecture at the University of California Los Angeles (UCLA), where he also worked as a teaching fellow in the Department of Architecture and Urban Design. During this time, he also collaborated with the Getty Research Institute and the Canadian Centre for Architecture. He previously studied at Università di Ferrara, the University of California Berkeley and TU Delft. He is the author of the book *The State of Architecture: Aldo Rossi and the Tools of Internationalization* (Poligrafo 2020) and multiple other writings, including articles for Architectural Histories, Ardeth, Footprint, Dune and Thresholds. The primary subject of study concerned the relation between architecture and power, focusing on the role of the state in the second half of the 20th century and the process of European integration.

1 Portrait of Sebastiano Fabbrini. Source: IUAV

Acknowledgments

Sebastiano Fabbrini passed away on June 16, 2024, at the age of 34, while he was working on the finalization of this book. This has been prepared for publication by his brother and parents, based on the precise notes we found in a detailed book proposal he had drafted. Sebastiano's work has been only minimally edited to correct typos and other formal inconsistencies.

As is common in academia, this book includes both original materials, including the Introduction and the Conclusion, as well as work that was previously published elsewhere, almost always open access. In particular, we wish to acknowledge that:

- Chapter 2 was published in (2021) 9 *Archimera* 151–166
- Chapter 3 appeared in (2020) 7 *Ardeth* 85–106
- Chapter 4 was published in (2023) 11(1) *Architectural Histories* 1–25
- Chapter 5 appeared in (2021) 9(1) *Architectural Histories* 1–18
- Chapter 6 was published in (2021) 2(1) *Dune* 24–33.

All material is reproduced here with full permission from the respective journals, which we thank for the support.

This volume is the testimony of a young man with a brilliant mind, a passion for architectural history, and a commitment to a united Europe.

Manuela Cescatti, Federico Fabbrini, Sergio Fabbrini

Table of Contents

Foreword

When I first met Sebastiano in 2013, as he began the MA program in the history of architecture at UCLA, he seemed to welcome the "New World" promises made to generations of "Old World" Italians in California with optimism. He spoke of his pleasure in being in the United States where, in contrast to Berlusconi's interminable reign of autocratic populism, Obama was finding unexpected success in his second term as president. Sebastiano also seemed a bit surprised to discover that the context gave new force to capacities already within himself; his classically Italian education, which instilled in him impeccable English and deep mastery of the canon of architectural figures and styles, also enabled him easily to maneuver the heterogenous array of subjects an exceedingly, if typically, diverse American faculty challenged him to confront. Nevertheless, the specific topics he chose to research over the course of his studies betray a deepening understanding of the costs of the myths of progress and of universalism quintessentially embedded in university culture. By the time he completed his PhD in 2018 and published *The State of Architecture; Aldo Rossi and the Tools of Internationalization,* Sebastiano's focus was on what he called the workings of an architect through which he linked Mussolini's Italy with Reagan's America, and the Communist Party to Disneyland. By examining architecture as work, in other words, rather than by interpreting the intentions or poetics of a canonic architect's work, Sebastiano had begun to unfold the radical instabilities that inhere within the myths needed to maintain the apparently smooth operations of power, particularly those reaching beyond single figures, institutions, or states.

As I write the foreword to this, Sebastiano's second and tragically his last book, Trump is about to assume the US presidency, again, Brexit is in place, Gaza is in ruins and the Ukraine at risk, developments that make this study of what Sebastiano brilliantly describes as the reluctant architecture of the European Union especially salient. Despite the potentially apocalyptic dangers of the current moment, the quasi-utopia that constitutes the European Union, a structure through which world wars gave way to new bonds, seems still to be holding. Sebastiano's careful and probing investigation into the causes of this persistence suggests that fragile design and the unenthusiastic exercise of power is the most robust and enduing response to the kinds of perpetual provocations that bedevil the world today. Sebastiano was ideally suited to explore the entangled histories that produce the design of power; like his mother, he was a student of architecture, while his father and brother are political scientists and legal scholars. I like to think, in other words, that the result of his nature and the world that nurtured him, was his marvelous discovery that the only good form of power is that which is shaped by reluctance.

Sebastiano's interest in reluctance offers an important model for contemporary historians of architecture. Sebastiano at first hesitated to give up the architect as the protagonist of architectural history, but in the all too few years I had the privilege of knowing him, he made extraordinary advances in reorienting the field from heroes to collectives, from buildings to territories, and from single states to supranational unions, as this splendid book reveals. Like many workers on the collective, Sebastiano did much of his work in isolation, both that wrought by scholarly practice and by the nature of human existential suffering. But he was also part of many collectives, of students at Ferrara and UCLA, of colleagues at the IUAV and throughout the field, of a family that loves and misses him, and of what will no doubt be the many unknown readers this important book will body forth and bring together.

Sylvia Lavin
Princeton, NJ
Dec. 2024

Chapter 1
Introduction: The Reluctant Architecture of the EU

The European Union (EU) is a unique experiment in shared governance, based on the principle of supra-nationalization: a voluntary transfer of power from a group of states to an entity that operates above them. While it is often viewed as a technocratic process, European integration is indeed an engine for cultural transformation, with wide-ranging implications. This book addresses this process from the prism of architecture, a discipline that has had close ties with power throughout history. Although the architectural discourse is frequently accused of Eurocentrism, very little attention has been devoted to European integration, the most significant shift in power dynamics on the old continent over the past seventy years. Since the start of the integration process in the 1950s, the establishment and expansion of European institutions has led to a substantial number of architectural productions, both built and imagined. Despite the power of these institutions, however, their architectural output is largely unknown and, when put under the microscope, comes across as unusual, idiosyncratic or altogether inadequate. Whereas national institutions rely heavily on architecture, embracing its ability to project power and shape political culture, the European institutions operate in a different way. The representational tools that architecture brings to the table are viewed as a problem, something to be minimized or avoided as much as possible. Researching this material, one simple question keeps coming up: why is it so difficult for the EU to engage with architecture?

This book theorizes a form of reluctance towards architecture and attempts to identify its underlying causes, addressing the tension between the national and the supranational, the historical bond between architecture and the state, the shortage of acceptable images of Europe, the processual *modus operandi* and the functionalist culture of the European institutions, as well as the legal constraints that have limited their operations in the built environment. Two institutions are particularly important: the European Commission and the European Central Bank, the two bodies that, together with the European Court of Justice, have been designed to operate on a supranational level. The book traces their workings over a significant timeframe, from the 1992 Maastricht Treaty to the economic crisis of the late-2000s. Three layers of analysis frame the structure of the book: buildings, images and policies. The first layer focuses on the buildings, the headquarters of the European Commission in

Brussels and the European Central Bank in Frankfurt. The second layer explores a key project, promoted by those institutions during the same time, that centered on the production of architectural images: the design of the Euro banknotes. The third layer examines how EU institutions influence the practice of architecture on a policy-level, mostly through funding, as well as through the introduction of rules, guidelines and incentives.

The common thread in these case studies is the need to maintain a low profile, focusing on performance rather than meaning. A constant concern of the EU is that, given the fragile nature of a supranational democracy, any overt projection of power may be perceived as overbearing or, even worse, illegitimate and generate a nationalist backlash. The book argues that, at the root of this impasse, is a political deficit. To borrow Jacques Delors's words, the EU has evolved into an economic giant but is still a political dwarf. For a multi-level, supranational union that responds to a model of depoliticized governance, institutional buildings and other forms of architectural representation constitute a minefield, as they bring about difficult political questions. Rather than embracing architecture as an instrument to generate identitarian symbols, the EU is reluctant to step into this field and, when it does, architecture must undergo a process of semantic neutralization. From this perspective, the European Union presents itself as a remarkable exception in the history of the relation between architecture and power, which this book sets out to explore and conceptualize.

The book stems from a long-term research project I conducted at IUAV University in Venice, started in 2019. It employs the methods and tools of architectural history. Most of the material derives from archival research in Brussels and Frankfurt (in the archives of the European institutions), as well as site visits and a few interviews. It is constructed as a rigorous, scientific product, whose primary audience will be the academic community in the field of architecture and urban design. Throughout the development of this project, the author has encountered a great deal of interest among other scientific communities as well. The book aims also to engage with other disciplines that focus on the EU and its dynamics. European integration has become one of the primary objects of study in the fields of political science, contemporary history, international relations, law, and economics, among others. The book wants to provide a different, original perspective on this object of study to scholars and students in these fields, looking at the EU through the prism of architecture. Moreover, given the importance of the EU in the broader cultural discourse, the book can also appeal to a wider, non-academic audience. Looking at European integration through the lens of architecture provides a unique opportunity not only to anchor the analysis of such incorporeal phenomenon to tangible objects, but also to obverse in the most direct way how things are shaped and built within our complex, supranational system. Finally, the book has an international reach, not yet covered by other scholars. This is also the most effective way to intersect a plurality of audiences across Europe, as well as outside of Europe.

Chapters Outline

The book traces a set of dynamics within a specific timeframe: from the Maastricht Treaty of 1992, when the European Union was established, to the Lisbon Treaty of 2007. It was a fifteen-year period of growth and optimism, which came to a halt in the mid-to-late 2000s, due to the failure to ratify a European constitution and the impact of the sovereign-debt crisis. This historical window is significant for multiple reasons. First, 1992 is the year in which a decision is finally taken, among the representatives of the member states, regarding the location of the European institutions. This meant that, for the first time, the European institutions had the legal authority to design, build and own their architecture. Second, as the integration process deepened and expanded, during this time the European institutions were surrounded by an aura of positivity and had enough leeway to start thinking about increasingly political questions, especially as it pertained to their image. Third, the chosen timeframe relates to the existing literature on this subject. Most of the (limited) scholarship on the EEC in the field of architecture and urban design focuses on the post-war years. The main, and really the only full-fledged historical study on the topic is Carola Hein's 2004 book *The Capital of Europe*, which provides an excellent account of the architectural and urban projects associated with the European economic community in the pre-Maastricht era. The present book sets out to build on this study and to explore the next phase of the integration process.

The book is structured around five chapters. All the chapters underline a ten sion between the national and the supranational, which heats up whenever the EU tries to put forward an image of itself. This is a key theme of the book, highlighted by the second chapter on "Against the plan". My analysis there follows two case studies that illuminate how this tension played out in the early part of the integration process: on the one hand, a set of unplanned buildings that marked the spontaneous entrenchment of Brussels as the primary seat of the European institutions; on the other hand, a set of unbuilt plans for a single European capital on the Franco-German border. European integration has been described and interpreted through a multitude of architectural metaphors, starting with Robert Schuman's declaration in favor of "concrete achievements" and against a "single plan." Moving out of the metaphorical dimension and beginning to examine the actual architecture produced by and for this system, there is a new opportunity to observe, through the lens of its most tangible outputs, how the European Union *builds*.

The third and fourth chapters focus primarily on the building of the European Commission in Brussels, known as the Berlaymont, and on the building of the European Central Bank (ECB) in Frankfurt. These institutions are significant because, more than any other, they embody the supranational ambition of the European project. The term "supranational" was first used in the context of the European Coal and Steel Community, as the legal concept chosen to characterize the method of integration. At the heart of this innovation was the idea that power, in addition to being shared between (*inter*) nations, needed to be transferred, in certain areas, to an entity above (*supra*) them. Even though the member states maintain an important role in the governance of the community, mainly through the European Council and the other intergovernmental fora, the underlying logic of the integration process is to gradually separate power from statecraft. It is worth remembering that this process began in the aftermath of World War II, as everyone had just witnessed the consequences of nationalism pushed to its limits. The space of the supranational, therefore, is not just a space where nations come together and pool some of their powers: it also entails a project of *nation-unbuilding*. This creates all sorts of problems vis-à-vis architecture, which has cut its political teeth, over centuries, in the project of state-building and nation-building. Now came an institution that could not employ those methods and, in addition to that, saw itself as a neutral, technical agent, with as little political representation as possible. Supra-nationalization and depoliticization are the two underlying dynamics that, feeding each other, make the EU such a unique, interesting proposition — one that raises difficult questions for architecture.

Berlaymont, the headquarter of the European Commission, is the first case in which these tensions came to the surface in a major way. The way the project was conceived and executed in the 1960s reflects the complex position of the European institutions before the Maastricht Treaty. As the Commission had a provisional status and limited agency over architectural matters, the Berlaymont, along with the rest of the European quarter in Brussels, including the European Parliament building, was produced by Belgian authorities in collaboration with local, private actors. While tracing this initial development, the third chapter of this book mostly focuses on a transformation that took place in the 1990s. Precisely as the status of the Commission was about to change, in 1991 the Berlaymont had to be evacuated due to the detection of large quantities of asbestos in the structure. The chapter examines the process of renovation, which ended up taking thirteen years, during which the Berlaymont was wrapped in a white protective canvas. The financing and management of the project were assigned to a consortium of private banks, while the Commission provided a set of guidelines, the embryo of what would become an architectural policy. The assignment was to project a "sober and functional" image, while focusing on the technical performance of the building. From this perspective, the new Berlaymont was also to operate as a test site for a new directive of the Commission on the energy performance of buildings. The main result was a façade system that, while providing high energy performance, had a fundamental problem: it allowed views from the inside out, but was opaque from the outside in, from the perspective of the citizens. The designers also stated that the new façade was meant to evoke the "purified white wrapping" used during the asbestos removal, which over time had become an iconic image.

The third chapter also considers the European Parliament premise in Brussels, known as the Spinelli building: the building was developed in secret, because the French government opposed moving the institution away from its initial seat, in Strasbourg. For the entirety of the development process, the massive complex that came to house the European Parliament in Brussels was camouflaged as an "international congress centre." Then, once the building was completed, the national decision-makers were presented with the *fait accompli* and pushed to make a deal, in order to allow some of the parliamentary activities to take place in Brussels. The effort was promoted and funded by a group of private investors, led by two Belgian banks, which commissioned the design to a local, 26-year-old architect.

If the cases of the Berlaymont and the Spinelli building shine light on the entrenchment of Brussels as a European center of power and the idiosyncrasies of the pre-Maastricht era, the other building studied in the book emerged in different circumstances. The fourth chapter focuses on the competition for the design of the headquarters of the ECB, in Frankfurt, which was launched in 2002. The two buildings of the European Commission and the ECB operate as framing devices for this book, as they reflect key developments at the two ends of the historical window under examination. Unlike the renovated Berlaymont, the building of the ECB had to house a brand-new institution, created in the late-1990s to oversee the most significant act of supra-nationalization: the creation of a common currency, the Euro. Many influential European architects took part in the competition, which was eventually won by Coop Himmelb(l)au. The competition documents show two interesting dynamics: on one hand, the institution framed the project in functional, utilitarian terms, as in the case of the Berlaymont renovation, and policed any proposal that could come across as a political statement; on the other hand, this functionalist outlook aligned with the approach of most of the participating architects. The traditional concern with representation had clearly given way to an evolving notion of materialism, which set aside questions of meaning in favor of questions of performance. The unfolding of the ECB project, however, revealed the limitations of such an approach. Given the importance of the bank within the governance of the European Union during a time of economic crisis, the building site became the stage for multiple symbolic rituals, political demonstrations and forced a difficult reflection on the image of the European community.

The cases of the Berlaymont and the ECB are interesting because they also allow an opportunity to establish a comparison with other institutional buildings. For example, the initial project of the Berlaymont was modelled after the UNESCO building in Paris and the Nestlé headquarters in Vevey, Switzerland. This is a unique chance to consider the differences between supranational, international and multinational organizations. Also, as the European Commission was set up in Brussels on a provisional basis, the Berlaymont was initially designed to host a ministry of the Belgian government, a national institution. The Belgian authorities did not want to make a large investment for an institution that might have left after a few years: the result was a building that never really fit the *modus operandi* of the Commission. On the other hand, the case of the ECB provides another key term of comparison. Here the model was the Bundesbank and, more broadly, the governmental architecture that had developed in Germany after World War II. After the trauma of Nazism, all German institutional buildings needed to maintain a low profile and avoid overt projections of power.

For different reasons, the EU has taken a similar approach. Operating in stealth-mode is regarded as the best way to avoid frictions with national bodies, which would struggle to accept an overt representation of their loss of power. When it comes to architecture, the goal is not to stand out, but to blend in.

The chapters on the buildings of the European Commission and the ECB are accompanied by two further chapters that examine efforts, by those very institutions, to produce architectural images of the EU. During the timeframe of this study, both institutions, while working on their buildings, were also engaged in the development of images.

The fifth chapter, specifically, relates to the ECB which, in the late-1990s, oversaw the most systematic attempt to elaborate a supranational image, using architectural elements. This chapter focuses on the development of the architectural images for the Euro banknotes. Since the launch of the design competition, the primary concern has been national bias. The obvious option of putting forward images of iconic buildings or monuments, such as the Parthenon or the Eiffel Tower, was off the table. In fact, it is almost impossible to find a monument that was not conceived according to or retroactively steeped in some kind of nationalist narrative. The alternative solution was to focus on "architectural styles," looking to provide, without specific reference to any given building, an overview of European architectural history. To this end, the ECB created a committee, tasked with producing a *sui-generis* survey of European architecture, more than 100 architectural images, that could serve as a reference for the competition participants. First, this material had to be sanitized, excluding all the buildings that could be perceived as too nationally biased or politically incorrect. Then, the designers were specifically instructed not to reproduce these objects but rather use them as possible starting points for operations of stylization. The task was to turn a history of specific buildings into a history of generic styles. The competition was won by Robert Kalina, with a set of architectural images that were described as "fictional" and "nation-neutral." The case of the Euro banknotes speaks to the difficulty of dislodging both architecture and history from the framework of the nation-state.

In addition to buildings and images, the book explores how the European institutions impact architecture on a policy level. The starting point for the sixth chapter on this topic is the exhibition *On-Site: New Architecture in Spain*, held at the Museum of Modern Art in 2006. The exhibition celebrated the rise of a new school of architecture in Spain in the 1990s. Despite this national connotation, however, most of the projects on display had been funded by the EU, of which Spain had become a member in 1986. This example shines a light on the impact of the European structural funds and the way they indirectly shaped transformations in the built environment. The European Commission and the ECB play a key role in this process, along with another important institution: the European Investment Bank. In addition to and in exchange for its financial backing, these institutions provide input on both the content and the method of design, creating a complex system of rules, incentives and rewards. The 1990s are also the period in which EU funding for architecture starts to go hand in hand with other programs and initiatives of the European institutions: the city agenda, the Eurocodes, the Mies van der Rohe Award and the Architect's Council of Europe. The goal of this chapter is to explore how the European institutions, while struggling to define their own buildings and images, set in motion a set of programs that gradually changed the financial and normative framework in which architecture was produced in most of the continent. As evidenced by the case of Spain, however, these actions unfolded in the background, indirectly, while the narrative was still tied to national terms.

Finally, the concluding chapter summarizes the core theme of the book and the troubles of building in the European Union. Due to its complex supranational dimension, the European Union occupies a unique position in the chessboard of global governance. Since the start of the integration process in the 1950s, the creation and expansion of the European institutions has led to the production of a substantial amount of architecture. Despite the power of these institutions, however, their buildings are largely unknown and, when put under the microscope, come across as wildly inadequate. Whereas national institutions rely heavily on architecture, embracing its ability to project power and shape political culture, supranational institutions operate in a different way. The representational tools that architecture brings to the table are viewed as a problem, something to be minimized or avoided as much as possible. This chapter focuses on why is it so difficult for the European institutions to engage with architecture and attempts to identify some of its underlying causes, addressing the tension between the national and the supranational, the historical bond between architecture and the state, the shortage of acceptable images of Europe, the processual *modus operandi* and the functionalist culture of the European institutions, as well as the legal constraints that have limited their operations in the built environment. At the root of this impasse is a political deficit. For a multi-level union that has evolved around a model of depoliticized governance, institutional buildings represent a challenge, as they may bring about unmanageable political questions. The transfer of power to the European sphere comes with a neutralization of architecture.

Chapter 2
Against the Plan: The Architecture of European Integration

Abstract

Although the architectural discourse has often been accused of being too Eurocentric and too politicized, we have mostly ignored the political dynamic that, more than any other, has been transforming the European archipelago over the past seventy years: European integration. Such dynamic subverts our common understanding of "the rear view," because it openly rejects planning and finality and, instead, unfolds as a gradual process, exploiting the spillovers and unintended consequences that occur when multiple states come together. The hypothesis that I have put to the test is that, in this unique, fragmented system, walking in a straight line, having a goal and knowing where to go — the features of Le Corbusier's planning method — undermine the possibility of building. On the contrary, the front views of this polity, the buildings in the limelight, result from a zigzag process, driven by contingency rather than planning. What is purposely designed as a front view tends to remain on paper due to a widespread concern for and distrust in the power of planning and, over time, that space is occupied by objects that respond to the logic of the rear view. My analysis follows two case studies that illuminate how this tension played out in the early part of the integration process: on the one hand, a set of unplanned buildings that marked the spontaneous entrenchment of Brussels as the primary seat of the European institutions; on the other hand, a set of unbuilt plans for a single European capital on the Franco-German border. European integration has been described and interpreted through a multitude of architectural metaphors, starting with Robert Schuman's declaration in favor of "concrete achievements" and against a "single plan." Moving out of the metaphorical dimension and beginning to examine the actual architecture produced by and for this system, there is a new opportunity to observe, through the lens of its most tangible outputs, how the European Union *builds*.

Europe's Rear View

This special issue of *archimaera* defines "the rear view" *(Rückseite)* as the unplanned or previously planned, what has come out of view, what has passed and is left behind.

It opposes the rear view to a series of concepts that relate to space, time and the way we move through them: straight line, one direction, destination, goal, plan. But it also pits it against broader social concepts, such as control, efficiency, clarity, visibility, perfection, progress. The editorial board appropriately chose Le Corbusier's famous metaphor of the pack-donkey to introduce such dichotomy.

Over the past year, I have conducted a research project on the architecture of a system that constantly challenges the way we are used to see the terms of this opposition, partly because it was developed in contrast to the *ethos* that underlaid Le Corbusier's theory. In this system, the front view—what has been built and is there for everyone to see—is the result of a process that, ironically, aligns with the description of the pack-donkey's way: "it meanders along, meditates a little in its scatter-brained and distracted fashion, zigzags in order to avoid the larger stones, or to ease the climb or to gain a little shade; it takes the line of least resistance."[1] On the other hand, the rear view—what has been dismissed and forgotten—is a repository of unbuilt plans that "walk in a straight line because they have a goal and know where they are going."[2]

The way this system is commonly introduced is through its founding statement—a declaration issued by another Frenchman, precisely 25 years after the publication of Le Corbusier's *The City of Tomorrow and its Planning*. Its pivotal passage reads as follows: "Europe will not be made all at once, or according to a single, general plan; it will be built through concrete achievements, which first create a *de facto* solidarity"[3] (Fig. 1). What is known as the Schuman declaration was delivered on May 9th, 1950, in the Salon de l'Horloge of the French Foreign Ministry in Paris; that day is still celebrated every year as the "Europe day." In fact, this statement became the basis for the foundation of the European Coal and Steel Community one year later, triggering the process of European integration.[4]

Written by Robert Schuman and Jean Monnet, who are often referred to as the "architects" of European integration, the declaration is the object of a vast literature. One of its key aspects, however, has been overlooked—an aspect that points directly to the question of the rear view: the first step in the construction of one of the most complex systems of our time was the explicit rejection of any overarching, comprehensive plan. Paradoxically, even though its core message was a statement

1 Le Corbusier: "The Pack-Donkey's Way and the Man's Way." In: idem, *The City of Tomorrow and its Planning*. New York 1987 [1925], p. 5.

2 Ibid, p. 5.

3 The full text of the Schuman declaration, along with the preparatory drafts and a recording of the speech, is available at the Centre Virtuel de la Connaissance sur l'Europe: https://www.cvce.eu/en/search?q=Schuman+Declaration.

4 For a comprehensive historical overview of the process of European integration, see Desmond Dinan (ed.): *Origins and Evolution of the European Union*. Oxford 2006; and Ivan Berend: *The History of European Integration*. London 2016.

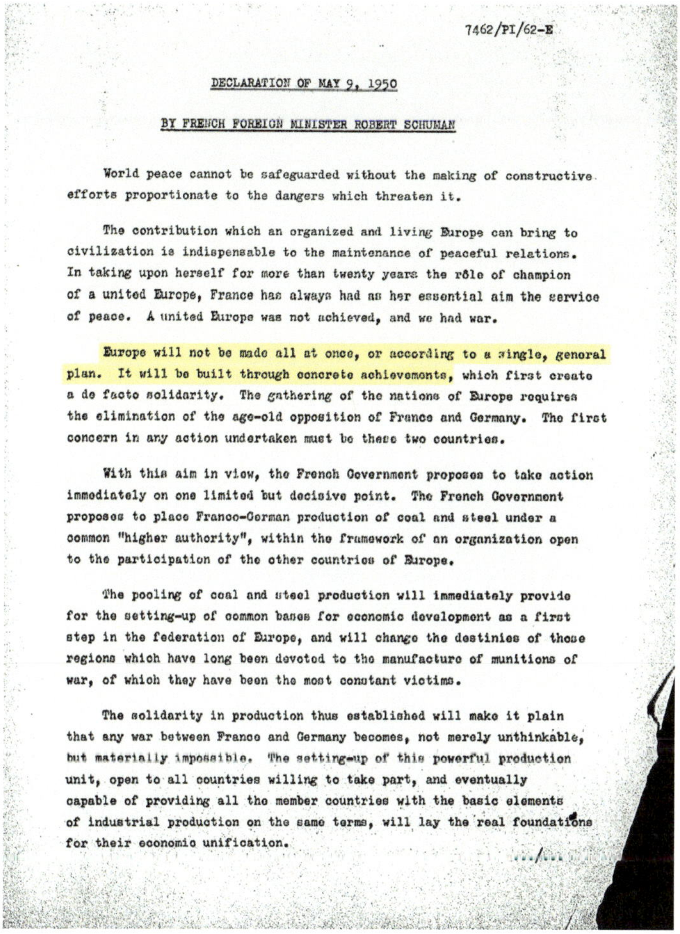

7462/PI/62-E

DECLARATION OF MAY 9, 1950

BY FRENCH FOREIGN MINISTER ROBERT SCHUMAN

World peace cannot be safeguarded without the making of constructive efforts proportionate to the dangers which threaten it.

The contribution which an organized and living Europe can bring to civilization is indispensable to the maintenance of peaceful relations. In taking upon herself for more than twenty years the rôle of champion of a united Europe, France has always had as her essential aim the service of peace. A united Europe was not achieved, and we had war.

Europe will not be made all at once, or according to a single, general plan. It will be built through concrete achievements, which first create a de facto solidarity. The gathering of the nations of Europe requires the elimination of the age-old opposition of France and Germany. The first concern in any action undertaken must be these two countries.

With this aim in view, the French Government proposes to take action immediately on one limited but decisive point. The French Government proposes to place Franco-German production of coal and steel under a common "higher authority", within the framework of an organization open to the participation of the other countries of Europe.

The pooling of coal and steel production will immediately provide for the setting-up of common bases for economic development as a first step in the federation of Europe, and will change the destinies of those regions which have long been devoted to the manufacture of munitions of war, of which they have been the most constant victims.

The solidarity in production thus established will make it plain that any war between France and Germany becomes, not merely unthinkable, but materially impossible. The setting-up of this powerful production unit, open to all countries willing to take part, and eventually capable of providing all the member countries with the basic elements of industrial production on the same terms, will lay the real foundations for their economic unification.

.../...

1 Transcript of the Schuman Declaration, 1950.
Source: Centre Virtuel de la Connaissance sur l'Europe.

against planning, the Schuman declaration is often improperly referred to as the Schuman plan.

It is important to remember that the context of this declaration was that of a shell-shocked continent pressed between two emerging powers, the United States and the Soviet Union, that had both embraced planning as a central tool of governance at home and abroad: in 1947, shortly before the establishment of the European Coal and Steel Community, the Marshall plan (Fig. 2) and the Molotov plan were put in place almost simultaneously to both provide aid and exert control over Europe's Western and Eastern blocs, respectively.

When a new polity is established, the cornerstone is usually a document called constitution, which, as noted by a multitude of political scientists, acts as a "general

2 Poster of the Marshall Pan, 1950.
Source: Marshall Foundation.

plan of government."[5] European integration never had such a plan and, when the first attempt was made at passing a constitutional treaty in 2004, it encountered major opposition and failed to be ratified.

Throughout the process of European integration, nearly every policy proposal that took the form of a plan, or was simply branded as a plan, ended up being redlighted: the list includes the Pleven plan, the Spaak plan, the Fouchet plan, the Tindemans plan, the Spinelli plan and the Giscard d'Estaing plan, among others. The latest example is the so-called "Recovery plan" designed to cope with the Coronavirus crisis, which has just been taken apart by the European Council.

Plan/Process

The term "plan" has multiple layers of meaning: it can indicate a set of decisions about how to do something in the future; it can designate a drawing from which something is made or built, as in the case of an architectural plan; but it also leads to the concept of planning, which, borrowing the Merriam-Webster definition, refers to "the establishment of goals, policies and procedures for a social or economic unit."[6]

5 William Barclay Allen and Kevin Cloonan: *The Federalist Papers. A Commentary*. New York 2000, p. 27.

6 "Planning." In: Merriam-Webster Dictionary: https://www.merriam-webster.com/dictionary/planning.

In his seminal book on the origins of modern town planning, Leonardo Benevolo started with a concept that he regarded as a simple truth: “planning is part of politics and is necessary to make any operational programme concrete.”[7] The building endeavors associated with European integration, however, point in a different direction. This is partly because one of the defining features of this system is a thinning of the political dimension: Zygmunt Bauman referred to it as a separation between power and politics.[8] But there is more to it.

Firstly, no attention has been devoted to the connection between the launch of the first European institutions in the 1950ies and what Anthony Fontenot has defined as a “history of non-planning”[9] — a movement that found its roots in the work of thinkers like Friedrich August Hayek and Bertrand Russell and, following the devastation of World War II, started to reassess plans as instruments of control and domination, associated with modern statehood and, most importantly, with its nationalist degenerations.

One of the most significant instances in which such association came to the fore was the Nuremberg trial, immediately after the war. Notably, the first two indictments were for “participation in a common plan or conspiracy for the accomplishment of a crime against peace” and “planning, initiating and waging wars of aggression.” In fact, the trial started with the projection of a short film, prepared by the American prosecutors, titled “The Nazi plan.”[10] In many ways, Nuremberg was framed as a process *(Prozess)* against a plan.

In the introduction to *The Road to Serfdom*, Hayek noted that “in order to achieve their ends, the planners must create power — power over men wielded by other men — so that it can be used in the service of a single plan.”[11] From his perspective, democracy and freedom were antithetical to any effort to establish a “single plan.” The illustrations that accompanied the book and appeared on *Look Magazine* in 1945 showed a direct correlation between the presentation of a plan and the emergence of a dictator with Mussolinian features (Fig. 3).

In the late 1930s, there was still hope in the possibility of “planning for freedom,” as Karl Mannheim put it. By the beginning of the war, however, the point of view had changed dramatically. In 1940, responding to Mannheim’s thoughts on the role of planning in a democratic society and its separation from the idea of *Gleichschaltung*, John Middleton Murry was rather categorical: “I see no solution except through a painful process of disintegration of our centralized societies.”[12]

7 Leonardo Benevolo: *Le Origini dell’Urbanistica Moderna*. Rome 1974 [1963], p. 10. Translated by the author.

8 Cf. Zygmunt Bauman: *State of Crisis*. Cambridge 2014.

9 Anthony Fontenot: “Notes Toward a History of Non-Planning.” In: *Places Journal* (2015).

10 Cf. Telford Taylor: *The Anatomy of the Nuremberg Trials*. New York 2013.

11 Friedrich August Hayek: *The Road to Serfdom*. London 2008 [1944], p. 165.

12 Jonas Kurlberg: *Christian Modernism in an Age of Totalitarianism. T. S. Eliot, Karl Mannheim and the Moot*. London 2019, p. 79. Mannheim’s reflections on this subject were published in the posthumous book *Freedom, Power and Democratic Planning*. Oxford 1950.

3 Illustrations of Friedrich August Hayek's The Road to Serfdom, 1945.
Source: Look Magazine.

As noted by Fontenot, architects and urbanists were very much involved in this reassessment of planning during the post-war period. The 1960s started with the publication of Jane Jacobs's reflections on the "failure of town planning" and ended with Robert Goodman's *After the Planners*.[13] During those years, Reyner Banham, Cedric Price, Peter Hall and Paul Barker collaborated on a manifesto titled *Non-Plan: An Experiment in Freedom*, which aimed to shine a light on environments that had been spontaneously shaped by their inhabitants.[14] For Banham, the "art of planning" was a "giant wastebin of sumptuously forgotten paper projects."[15]

In *Planning in Postmodern Times*, Philip Allmendinger associated this "growth in anti-planning thinking" with the process of postmodernization.[16] Simultaneously, Peter van Ham published the first book that discussed European integration in relation to "the postmodern condition," following Robert Cooper's famous definition of the European Union as "the most developed example of a postmodern system."[17] Allmendinger argued that, while planning was deeply submerged in the practices of

13 Cf. Jane Jacobs: *The Death and Life of Great American Cities. The Failure of Town Planning*. New York 1961; and Robert Goodman: *After the Planners*. New York 1971.

14 Cf. Reyner Banham, Cedric Price, Peter Hall and Paul Barker: "Non-Plan: An Experiment in Freedom." In: *New Society*, 20 March 1969, pp. 435–443.

15 Reyner Banham: *Los Angeles. The Architecture of Four Ecologies*. Los Angeles 2009 [1971], p. 119.

16 Philip Allmendinger: *Planning in Postmodern Times*. London 2001, p. 4.

17 Peter van Ham: *European Integration and the Postmodern Condition. Governance, Democracy, Identity*. London 2001, p. ix; and Robert Cooper: *The Postmodern State and the World Order*. London 1996, p. 24.

modernity, postmodernization brought about "the more decentered view that we can never represent reality and instead must accept a never-ending chain of signifiers."[18]

The notion of a "never-ending chain" points to a key term: although there are many different interpretations of European integration, the one aspect on which everyone agrees is that it constitutes a "process."[19] This is far from being a neutral, value-free characterization, as thinking in terms of "processes" relates to specific ideological *milieux*. For example, Daniel Dombrowski and Randall Morris have highlighted the interconnection between process philosophy and political liberalism.[20] Furthermore, it relates to contemporaneous developments in technology: with the advent of the digital, every interaction between humans and digital applications started to go through a little machine called "processor," often referred to as a computer's brain.

In spite of the reference to "an ever-closer union" in the Treaty establishing the European Community, the defining feature of European integration has been the lack of a clear goal. In the literature, this topic is addressed as the issue of "finality."[21] As noted by Ulrich Haltern, "the Schuman declaration left the question of Europe's ends unanswered" and this void was never filled in the following decades.[22] In his influential speech *Thoughts on the Finality of European Integration*, Joschka Fischer described the unification of Europe as "a gradual process with no blueprint for the final state," that is a process without a plan.[23]

Unbuilt/Built

Understanding this divergence between the concepts of "plan" and "process" is key to our analysis of European integration and its architecture. We usually look at the lack of planning as an accident or a frustrating shortcoming, but the perspective changes when we start to see it as an underlying condition. The opposition between the front view and the rear view is part of the same tension: what Le Corbusier called the "man's way" is a definition of planning, while the way his pack-donkey moved can easily be read as a process without a plan.

18 Philip Allmendinger: *Planning in Postmodern Times*. London 2001, p. 20.
19 Cf. Antje Wiener and Thomas Diez (Eds.): *European Integration Theory*. Oxford 2004.
20 Cf. Daniel Dombrowski: *Process Philosophy and Political Liberalism*. Edinburgh 2019; and Randall Morris: *Process Philosophy and Political Ideology*. New York 1991.
21 Christian Rieck: "Quid est Europa? Myth, Finality, Utopia and the European Dream." In: Report of the Konrad Adenauer Stiftung, Berlin 2006.
22 Ulrich Haltern: "On Finality." In: Armin von Bogdandy and Jurgen Bast (Eds.): *Principles of European Constitutional Law*. Oxford 2009, p. 205.
23 Joschka Fischer: *From Confederacy to Federation. Thoughts on the Finality of European Integration*. Speech delivered in Berlin, 12 May 2000. European Commission — Documentation et Recherche sur les Questions Institutionnelles Européennes: https://ec.europa.eu/dorie/cardPrint.do?cardId=192161.

Nowhere is this tension more visible than in the field of architecture and urban design. Even though Umberto Eco famously argued that European integration should "deal with soft, not hard, stuff," a very significant amount of architectural hardware has been designed for the European institutions since the Schuman declaration.[24] In the most comprehensive historical study on this subject, Carola Hein divided this material into two streams: "Imagining built Europe," which focused on visionary, unrealized projects, and "Building imagined Europe," which instead addressed the concrete achievements.[25]

Removing all additional connotations, the fundamental divergence lays between built and unbuilt projects — a classification that can help us understand how the European Union operates (or does not operate) as a builder. Moving upstream through these two lines of inquiry, I have been testing a hypothesis that revolves around planning, or the lack thereof. The architectural and urban ideas that turned into buildings had, for the most part, one thing in common: they lacked a single plan. Those that had one, on the contrary, remained on paper.

Brussels

Brussels has been the epicenter of the building activities associated with European integration since the late 1950s. The headquarters of the two most important supranational institutions, the European Commission and the European Parliament, provide an interesting window into the question of planning.

The Berlaymont, the building of the Commission, originally had an open-plan layout because it was meant to host a Belgian ministry and, as soon as it was completed in 1968, it had to be entirely reorganized in order to accommodate the new European offices (Fig. 4), before the detection of asbestos forced a second transformation of the plan a few years later.[26] In the case of the Parliament, the plan operated as a decoy: the hemicycle was built under the radar, using the false name "Centre International de Conférences," because the official seat of the Parliament had already been established in Strasbourg (Fig. 5). The plan was carefully crafted to make the hemicycle look like something else, namely a regular congress center.[27]

24 Umberto Eco: "Soft Capital." In: European Commission: *Brussels, Capital of Europe*, Final Report, October 2001. European Quarter Fund: http://www.fondseuropesewijk.eu/Brussels%20capital%20of%20europe_final_report.pdf.

25 Carola Hein: *The Capital of Europe. Architecture and Urban Planning for the European Union*. Wesport 2004, p. 2.

26 Sven Sterken: "Le Berlaymont et la Transformation du Quartier Leopold." In: *Journées du Patrimoine Région de Bruxelles-Capitale* 15 (2009), pp. 102–117.

27 Cf. Ludovic Lamant: "Ceci n'est pas un Parlement." In: idem: *Bruxelles Chantiers. Une Critique Architectural de l'Europe*. Montreal 2018, pp. 117–142.

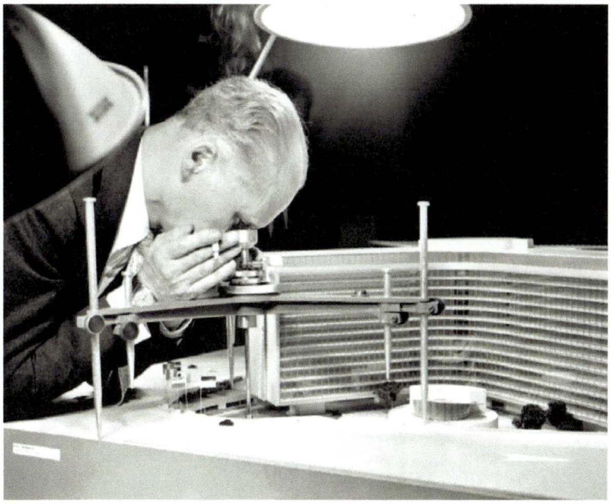

4 Design of the interiors of the Berlaymont, early 1960s.
Source: Ministère des Travaux Publics de Belgique.

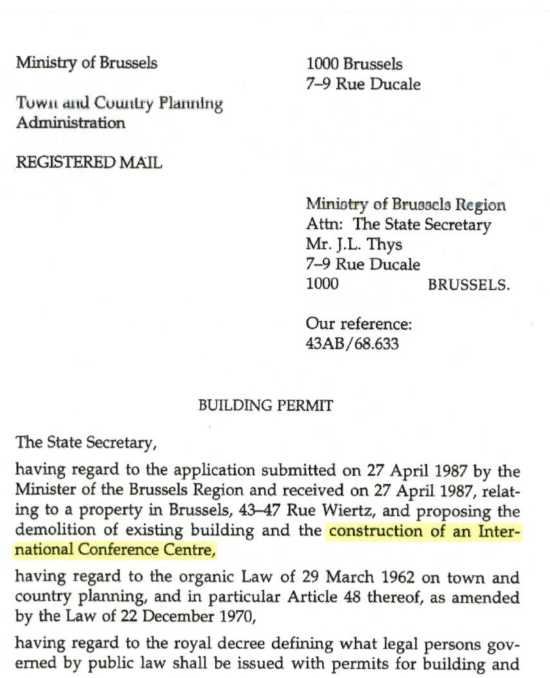

Ministry of Brussels

Town and Country Planning Administration

REGISTERED MAIL

1000 Brussels
7–9 Rue Ducale

Ministry of Brussels Region
Attn: The State Secretary
Mr. J.L. Thys
7–9 Rue Ducale
1000 BRUSSELS.

Our reference:
43AB/68.633

BUILDING PERMIT

The State Secretary,

having regard to the application submitted on 27 April 1987 by the Minister of the Brussels Region and received on 27 April 1987, relating to a property in Brussels, 43–47 Rue Wiertz, and proposing the demolition of existing building and the construction of an International Conference Centre,

having regard to the organic Law of 29 March 1962 on town and country planning, and in particular Article 48 thereof, as amended by the Law of 22 December 1970,

having regard to the royal decree defining what legal persons governed by public law shall be issued with permits for building and

5 Building permit for the headquarters of the European Parliament in Brussels, disguised as an "International Conference Centre," 1987.
Source: Alex Papadopoulos: Urban Strategies and Regimes.

Shifting the focus from the architectural scale to the urban scale, the history of Brussels as a European capital is characterized by an underlying absence of planning: in his book on Europe's central executive district, Alex Papadopoulos described the city's approach to planning as "nonexistent."[28] Even the decision to start using Brussels as a seat for the European institutions in 1958 was not based on a plan, but rather on the fact that it was the capital of the member state that preceded all the others in alphabetical order.[29]

In this early stage, the Belgian government did produce a plan, highlighting multiple locations in which the institutions could be placed: in spite of this, the European institutions ended up occupying one of the few areas that were not indicated in the plan, the Quartier Leopold, following a spontaneous expansion pattern, mostly driven by private developers.[30]

At the core of these dynamics was a fundamental issue of agency: until the Maastricht Treaty, Brussels (along with Strasbourg and Luxembourg) was only a provisional seat of the institutions, which therefore did not have legal authority to own, finance or design their buildings. Behind this prolonged provisional status was the idea to build, sooner or later, a European federal district on the model of Washington DC—a plan that was eventually abandoned in 1992.[31]

This vision was known as the "Monnet doctrine," because it had initially been promoted by Jean Monnet, seemingly contradicting the logic of the Schuman declaration and its stance against any centralization of power. In a report written after one of the first Council of Ministers of the European Coal and Steel Community, he put it this way: "I had no preference for one place in Europe rather than another. All that mattered to me was that it should be the site of all the institutions and that it should become a European territory, the embryo of an eventual federal district. There was nothing utopian about this proposal."[32]

Wissembourg

Before Brussels became the *de facto* center of the union, focalizing most of its architectural productions, multiple plans were drafted in response to Monnet's idea. None of these proposals came even close to being built, partly because no political consensus

28 Alex Papadopoulos: *Urban Regimes and Strategies. Building Europe's Central Executive District in Brussels.* Chicago 1996, p. 15

29 Cf. Philippe Van Parijs: "Why did Brussels become the capital of Europe? Because Belgium starts with letter B." In: Bxl Connect 9 (2014), pp. 6–8.

30 Cf. Michel de Beule (ed.): *Bruxelles, Histoire de Planifier. Urbanisme aux 19e et 20e Siècles.* Brussels 2017.

31 Cf. Koen Lenaerts and Kristien Vanvoorden: "The Legal Status of Brussels as European Capital." In: Roel De Groof (ed.): *Brussels and Europe.* Brussels 2008, pp. 127–152.

32 Jean Monnet: *Memoirs.* London 2015 [1976], p. 369.

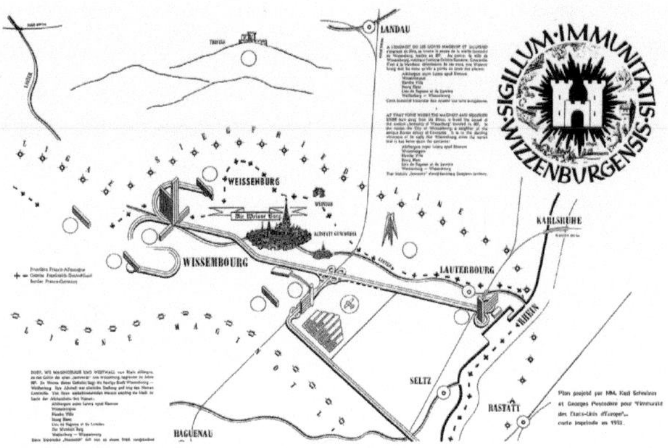

6 Karl-Oswald Schreiner & Georges-Henri Pescadére, plwan für Weiße Burg / Bourg Blanc, 1952.
Source: Citizens for Europe.

was ever found among the member states on the selection of a single site. As such, this is the ideal testing ground as it pertains to the tension between the presence of planning and the possibility of building.

Putting aside the proposals that have little to do with a supranational logic—such as the proposal known as *Paris Parallèle*, which imagined an extension of Paris as the center of a French Europe[33]—three plans produced in the early stages of European integration are particularly significant. They were all developed between the early 1950s and the early 1960s, in the space of less than thirty kilometers on the border between France and Germany.[34]

The first proposal centered on the Alsatian city of Wissembourg. In 1949, German journalist Karl-Oswald Schreiner and French painter Georges-Henri Pescadére, who had met as prisoners of the Nazis during the war, started to work on a plan for a transnational district on the border between their two countries, an area framed by the former Siegfried and Maginot lines, which were the two lines of fortification that Germany and France had built to combat each other (Fig. 6).[35] Schreiner and Pescadére were supported by the mayor of Wissembourg, who offered to provide land near the existing city and, most importantly, they obtained funding from the Marshall plan: the United States were very supportive of this type of endeavors because they saw the unification of Europe as a powerful tool in the struggle against the Soviets.

33 Cf. Claude Parent, "Paris Parallèle." In: *Architecture d'Aujourd'hui* 138 (1968), p. 17.
34 For an overview of these plans, see Carola Hein: "Urban Visions and Architectural Symbols for a United Europe, 1945–1968." In: idem: *The Capital of Europe. Architecture and Urban Planning for the European Union.* Westport 2004, pp. 39–66.
35 The documentation for this case study is available on the platform Citizens for Europe: https://www.citizens-4-europe.eu/index.php/en/themes/capital-for-europe.

The proposal had a strong symbolic connotation, since both envisioned this new capital, which they called Weiße Burg/Bourg Blanc (meaning "White City"), as a materialization of Europe's pacification.[36] At the heart of their plan was a major building intended as a place where young people from all over Europe could meet, get to know each other and learn to live together in peace. Nevertheless, the idea was to avoid any form of monumentality, as Schreiner and Pescadére associated the latter with the architecture of totalitarian regimes. From this perspective, the approach was like the one followed in the German capital Bonn in the same period.

The plan of the "White City" was evaluated by the European Coal and Steel Community in 1952. In order to make it happen, both Germany and France needed to give up a little bit of land and agree to create a transnational district. In the context of post-war Europe, ceding land was one of the most difficult and problematic actions to take. Neither Germany nor France, for different reasons, were willing to do it. Moreover, shortly afterwards, the funding of the Marshall plan came to an end, effectively closing this window of opportunity.[37]

Saarland

One year later, however, this endeavor inspired the launch of a competition for the planning of a European capital in the small region of the Saarland, a few kilometers north of Wissembourg on the Franco-German border.[38] After having heard the Schuman declaration, the local mayor Peter Zimmer sent a letter to Robert Schuman, offering his city as the site of the new institutions (Fig. 7): "I would like to ask the Conference to examine our proposal to choose Saarbrücken as the seat of the institutions of the European Coal and Steel Community and to allow us to submit detailed documentation with plans and supporting proposals for the construction of the envisaged buildings."[39]

Even though he never received a response, in 1953 the mayor organized a competition, calling for plans to turn the Saarland into a European district, on the model of the District of Columbia in the United States. The competition was overseen by local

36 Cf. Karl-Oswald Schreiner and Georges-Henri Pescadére: *Die Weisse Burg: Wissembourg en Alsace — Weißenburg im Elsaß*. Paris and Bad Godesberg, 1952.

37 Cf. Bernard Weigel: "Wissembourg: Le Projet du Bourg Blanc, 1952–1954." In: *L'Outre Foret* 60 (1986), pp. 28–36.

38 The documentation for this case study is available in the Open Gallery of the Landesarchiv Saarbrücken — Staatskanzlei des Saarlandes: https://artsandculture.google.com/exhibit/das-saarland-eine-europ%C3%A4ische-geschichte/wQjUon8c?hl=de.

39 The letter that mayor Peter Zimmer sent to Robert Schuman on 11 June 1951 is available at the Centre Virtuel de la Connaissance sur l'Europe: https://www.cvce.eu/en/obj/letter_of_application_of_the_city_of_saarbrucken_to_house_the_community_institutions_saarbrucken_11_june_1951-en-6f8eec29-6f25-4da2-b48a-3eb54c32092e.html.

7 Poster of the letter sent to Robert Schuman by the mayor of Saarbrücken, 1951.
Source: Landesarchiv Saarbrücken.

8 Cover of the exhibition catalogue of the Saarland competition, 1954.
Source: Landesarchiv Saarbrücken.

architect Otto Renner, who had worked in Le Corbusier's office and collaborated with Albert Speer before the war. Thirty-four proposals were presented, mostly coming from German and French architects and planners (Fig. 8).[40]

The anti-monumental sensibility that had characterized the plan for Wissembourg did not transfer to the Saarland competition. Examining the three entries that were awarded prizes by the jury, the one that stands out was the plan developed by French architects Henri Colboc and Pierre Dalidet, who proposed to group all the new European institutions in an enormous ring-shaped building, three hundred meters in diameter, connected to the existing city of Saarbrücken by a monumental boulevard on a sloping ramp (Fig. 9).[41]

The reasoning behind the Saarland competition was that, due to its complex history, this region had effectively blurred the border between Germany and France, if only because it had been razed to the ground almost every time the two countries had gone to war against each other. After World War I, the Saarland had become an international territory administered by the League of Nations, until the Nazis in-

40 Cf. "Wettbewerb Montanunionstadt Saarbrücken." In: *Bauwelt* 42 (1955), p. 838.
41 Ibid.

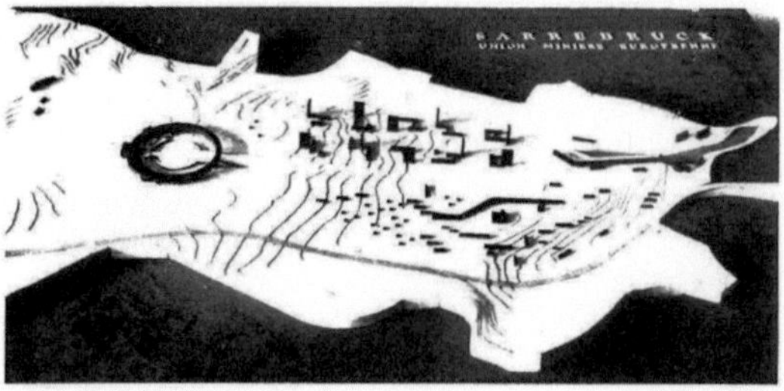

Bild 1. Ein erster Preis: Architekten Henri Colboc und Georges Philippe, Paris

Wettbewerb Montanunionstadt Saarbrücken

Bilder 2 bis 4. Zwei ebenfalls mit ersten Preisen ausgezeichnete Arbeiten: Professor Rudolf Krüger, Saarbrücken, und Oberbaurat Erich Stoll, Stuttgart (Bild 2); Dipl.-Ing. Gerhard Kilper, Stuttgart, Architekt Kurt Baldauf, Dillingen, Architekt Erwin Klein, Saarlouis, und Architekt Klaus Hoffmann, Saarlouis-Fraulautern (Bilder 3 und 4). Bild 4 zeigt ein Ausschnittmodell

In diesen Wochen des politischen Kampfes steht naturgemäß ein städtebaulicher Wettbewerb, der sich mit der Zukunft des Saarlandes und seiner Hauptstadt Saarbrücken als Sitz der Montanunion befaßt, im Vordergrund auch des fachlichen Interesses. Die Unterlagen des Wettbewerbes wurden von Oberregierungs- und Baurat Dipl.-Ing. Jäger und Architekt Dipl.-Ing. Otto Renner bearbeitet, fachliche Preisrichter waren Professor Werner Hebebrand, Hamburg, J. P. Oud, Rotterdam, G. A. Pingusson, Paris, Annibale Vittelozzi, Rom, aus Saarbrücken Fritz Ahammer, Wilhelm Feien, Hans Hirner, Ernst Höfer, Otto Renner und Bernhard Schultheis. Über das Ergebnis hat die Bauwelt in Heft 25/1955 berichtet, hier folgen Bilder der ersten drei Arbeiten. Wir entnehmen dem „Bau-Anzeiger für das Saarland" (Heft 26/1955) die folgenden Beurteilungen.

*

Bild 2

Ein erster Preis (Bild 1):

Henri Colboc und Georges Philippe, zwei Pariser Architekten, haben in der Mitte der von Hügeln eingerahmten Talmulde zwischen Tabaksweiher und Metzer Straße einen ringförmigen Baukörper als Dominante vorgesehen, der den ganzen Raum beherrscht und ihm seinen Stempel aufdrückt. Der von diesem Rundbau eingerahmte runde Platz übertrifft in seinen Ausmaßen noch den Petersplatz in Rom. Das Gebäude schafft durch seine konzentrierte Baumasse einen wesentlichen Kontrast zur aufgelockerten Stadtrandbebauung von Saarbrücken.

Bilder 3 und 4

Ein erster Preis (Bild 2):

Professor Rudolf Krüger, Saarbrücken, und Oberbaurat Erich Stoll, Stuttgart, lassen die Verwaltungsgebäude der Montanunion dadurch besonders hervortreten, daß sie auf einer Anhöhe innerhalb der Talmulde großzügig und großräumig angeordnet werden. Diese starke städtebauliche Dominante findet in der Zuordnung der Verwaltungsgebäude für die übrigen europäischen Einrichtungen eine naturgemäße Fortsetzung sowohl nach Westen als auch nach Osten. An diese Einrichtungen schließen sich die Wohngebiete an.

Ein erster Preis (Bilder 3 und 4):

Dipl.-Ing. Gerhard Kilper, Stuttgart, Architekt Kurt Baldauf, Dillingen, Architekt Erwin Klein, Saarlouis, und Architekt Klaus Hoffmann, Saarlouis-Fraulautern, setzen die Bauten der Montanunion als Kopf der Anlage auf die höchste Bodenerhebung und ordnen die anderen Institutionen entlang dem geschwungenen Höhenzug bis zum Tabaksmühlental an. Es bleiben nicht nur große Grünanlagen und Wasserflächen frei, sondern es wird auch Raum für eine Ausdehnung der Stadt Saarbrücken gewonnen.

838 BAUWELT 1955 HEFT 42

9 Bauwelt report on the Saarland competition, 1955.
Source: Bauwelt.

vaded it in the mid-1930s and, considering it an important symbolic site, turned it into the capital of the so-called Westmark region. Then, after it was devasted again during World War II, the Saarland became part of the French occupation zone in Germany.[42]

In both post-war periods, Germany and France laid claim to this territory by developing and partly implementing grand, comprehensive plans for Saarbrücken, approaching it as a blank slate and building representations of their dominant presence. While the German plans of the late-1930s were defined by a monumental neoclassicism, the French plans of the late-1940s were explicitly modelled after Le Corbusier's Ville Radieuse and aimed to "modernize" the city.[43]

Given the difficulty of positioning the Saarland in the geopolitical order that had emerged after the war, in 1954 the German and French governments started to discuss the idea of turning it into a supranational, European territory, and shortly afterwards asked the local citizens to decide on it. In a referendum held in 1955, however, a majority of the citizens of the Saarland voted against such proposed Europeanization and, as most of them had a German background, asked to be annexed by Germany.[44] As soon as Saarbrücken became a German city again, the planning competition, which was about to enter its second stage, came to an end. For obvious reasons, the capital of a new united Europe could not be located on German soil.

Lake Europa

After the abortion of the plans for Wissembourg and the Saarland, in the late-1950s a third proposal started to take shape in the same area, this time in Luxembourg, near the city of Schengen. This plan not only relied on American funding, like Schreiner's and Pescadére's "White City," but was also developed by an American planner: James Marshall Miller. A professor of planning at Columbia University, Miller elaborated a highly symbolic proposal for a European capital called "Lake Europa." With the support of the American committee of the International Federation for Housing and Planning and funding from the Ford Foundation, he made several trips to Europe in the 1950s and became deeply involved in the cause of European integration. A paci-

42 Cf. Wolfgang Behringer and Gabriele Clemens: *Geschichte des Saarlandes*. Munich 2009.

43 Cf. Marlen Dittmann: "100 Jahre Stadtplanung in Saarbrücken." Institut für Aktuelle Kunst im Saarland: http://institut-aktuelle-kunst.de/kunstlexikon/aspekte-100-jahre-stadtplanung-in-saarbruecken-1818; and Dietmar Kolling: "Saarbrücken, Pingusson, Aufbauplan und Französische Botschaft." Institut für Aktuelle Kunst im Saarland: http://institut-aktuelle-kunst.de/kunstlexikon/saarbruecken-pingusson-aufbauplan-und-franzoesische-botschaft-1977.

44 Cf. Bronson Long: *No Easy Occupation. French Control of the German Saar, 1944–1957*. Rochester 2015.

10 James Marshall Miller, plan for Lake Europa, 1963.
Source: Lake Europa. A New Capital for a United Europe.

fist and fervent anti-communist, Miller was an enthusiastic supporter of the integration process.[45]

After it had been introduced to an audience of planners at a seminar in The Hague in 1958, the project for "Lake Europa" was published in an eponymous book, produced by Miller himself in 1963,[46] while the construction of the Berlaymont in Brussels had just begun. This was certainly the most radical and symbolic proposal for a supranational capital. Its name referred to the idea of building a city on the shores of a new artificial lake, created at the juncture of Germany, France and Luxembourg—a lake that was to be supplied by the water of all the major European rivers (Fig. 10).

In spite of the naïveté of the proposal, Miller's book addressed in detail every aspect of its development, even the most technical, utilitarian issues, as if it was an ordinary endeavor. For example, a section of the book was devoted to explaining how the construction of "Lake Europa" could be funded. Miller imagined the creation of a semi-public corporation called "Lake Europa Development Authority" that could manage the project and draw the necessary financial resources. As the project required thousands of kilometers of pipes in order to transfer water from all over Europe, the idea was to ask major producers of pipes and oil companies (which possess "both the equipment and the skilled workers" necessary to lay said pipes[47]) to invest in this enterprise.

45 Cf. Philip Wagner: "James Marshall Miller, Champion of Transatlantic Urban Planning." In: *Transatlantic Perspectives*, 17 December 2013.
46 James Marshall Miller: *Lake Europa. A New Capital for a United Europe*. New York 1963.
47 Ibid., pp. 81–84.

Representatives of old and new world cooperate in building "altar" marking the site of "Lake Europa." Mr. Roger Krieps, of the Luxembourg newspaper *d'Letzeburger Land* and Prof. Miller lay first stones of monument near the Mosel River at the junction of the countries of Luxembourg, France, and Germany. 8 September 1961.

Prof. Miller addressing group at "pre-dedication ceremony" at site of proposed new European capital, "Lake Europa." 8 September 1961.

European and American pledge cooperation in pursuit of European unity. M. Pierre Wallerich, a resident in the area of the proposed European capital of "Lake Europa" and Prof. Miller exchange greetings at conclusion of "pre-dedication ceremony" at site of proposed metropolis. 8 September 1961.

(*Photos by Tony Krier*)

103

11 James Marshall Miller at the "pre-dedication ceremony" of Lake Europa, 1961. Source: Lake Europa. A New Capital for a United Europe.

Even though Miller attempted multiple times to pitch his idea to the European institutions, no one took him seriously. Nevertheless, on September 8, 1961, followed by a small crowd of local residents, a few American associates and a journalist from Luxembourg, Miller organized a ceremony for the laying of the first stone (Fig. 11). He described it as a "pre-dedication ceremony at the site of the proposed new European capital."[48] The participants assembled a few blocks of stone to form a make-shift altar, on which Miller attached a sign that he had brought from New York, which simply read "Lake Europa."

48 Cf. Robert Philippart: "Mittelpunkt eines geeinten Europas: Als Schengen Hauptstadt Westeuropas werden sollte." In: *Tageblatt Lëtzebuerg*, 24 July 2019: https://www.tageblatt.lu/headlines/mittelpunkt-eines-geeinten-europas-als-schengen-hauptstadt-westeuropas-werden-sollte/.

The Power of the Front View

Although the first sentence in the preface of Miller's book stressed that the objective was not to "outline a plan" but rather to "set forth an idea,"[49] his proposal—like those for Wissembourg and the Saarland—had all the features of a plan: it indicated a destination and, however unrealistic and naïve it may have been, a straight line to get there. In addition to being unbuilt, these proposals shared a similar approach: they "solved" the problem with a single gesture, they laid out an omni-comprehensive vision of the site at hand, they were not amenable to be modified and, fittingly, they were mostly drawn in plan. Moreover, they all reflected a clear vision of what European integration was and had to become: the capital city was designed to act as a materialization and a symbolic representation of that political idea.

Other equally, if not more utopian, plans had been elaborated in the first half of the twentieth century. In the second half of the 1920s, for example, Herman Sörgel had famously put forward a radical proposal to restructure the entire continent *(Atlantropa)*, going as far as to suggest draining part of the Mediterranean in order to claim new land and facilitate the connection with Africa.[50] What is different about the unbuilt proposals of the post-war period, however, is the fact that, rather than responding to a generic, ill-defined pan-Europeanism with marginal reach and influence, they were entrenched in a process that had actually started to change Europe. They responded to an idea that, although it was rapidly overcome by a more pragmatic, functionalist approach towards integration, had played a key role in its definition and activation: the idea of building a form of United States of Europe.[51]

In Carola Hein's study, the "urban visions and architectural symbols for a united Europe" developed in the two decades following World War II are associated with the emergence of "a strong trust in the power of planning."[52] While this trust was certainly at play in the post-war efforts of other systems, both to the West and the East of the old continent, the way European integration moved forward revealed, instead, a deep con-

49 James Marshall Miller: *Lake Europa: A New Capital for a United Europe*, New. York 1963, p. 1.

50 On Herman Sörgel's plan for Atlantropa or Panropa, see Peo Hansen and Stefan Jonsson: *Eurafrica. The Untold History of European Integration and Colonialism*. London 2015.

51 While this term had been circulating for decades, it took on a different meaning after World War II. For example, in a consequential speech delivered in 1946, Winston Churchill explicitly argued for the formation of "a kind of United States of Europe" (International Churchill Society: https://winstonchurchill.org/resources/speeches/1946-1963-elder-statesman/united-states-of-europe/). But the real force behind this idea was the federalist movement, led by Altiero Spinelli, who played a central role in laying the foundations of the integration process.

52 Carola Hein: "Urban Visions and Architectural Symbols for a United Europe, 1945–1968." In: idem: *The Capital of Europe. Architecture and Urban Planning for the European Union*. Westport 2004, p. 39.

cern and apprehension about the power of planning. For this, the case of the Saarland is particularly emblematic: having already experienced the power of planning on multiple occasions throughout their history, the Saar citizens voted against a proposal that, once again, involved a comprehensive, top-down plan that would have radically transformed their lives.

Jean Monnet himself was very familiar with this subject. Immediately after the end of World War II, he was appointed Commissioner-General of the French National Planning Board and was responsible for elaborating the plan for the economic reconstruction of his country.[53] But European integration operated in a different way: its underlying sentiment was a profound distrust towards planning.

Because of its complicated history, Brussels aligned perfectly with this change of pace. As noted by Ian Buruma, for much of its history, Brussels was occupied by oppressive empires and, when Belgium finally became independent in the nineteenth century, it found itself in the difficult position of being the capital of a fragmented nation, made of three very different linguistic and cultural communities.[54] In this framework, no single, centralized plan could ever be accepted and implemented.

According to Pier Vittorio Aureli, since the establishment of the European institutions "absolutely no official plan has ever existed" regarding their urban and architectural integration in Brussels.[55] Philippe Van Parijs described the entrenchment of Brussels as the capital of Europe as a "massive snowball process."[56] From this point of view, Brussels can be read as the unsung antithesis to the eminent planned capitals of the 1950s, from Chandigarh to Brasília. Maristella Casciato and Stanislaus von Moos have described these efforts as "the twilight of the plan."[57] But no attention has been paid to the fact that, while the European, modernist approach towards urbanism was having its twilight overseas, with Le Corbusier leading the charge, the new capital of Europe was being built in a diametrically different fashion, navigating the problems as well as the opportunities of the unplanned.

Nevertheless, Brussels has unequivocally become the front view of the European Union. The Berlaymont is a fitting example: it is hard to find a news story about European integration that does not include images of this building—one that was constructed without even knowing what type of institution it would host. Aptly, in the mid-2000s, when the European Commission had to develop a logo—the quintessential front view—the choice fell on a stylized image of the silhouette of the

53 Cf. François Duchene: *Jean Monnet. The First Statesman of Interdependence.* New York 1994.

54 Ian Buruma: "In the Capital of Europe." In: *The New York Review of Books*, 7 April 2016, pp. 36–39.

55 Pier Vittorio Aureli (ed.): *Brussels, a Manifesto. Towards the Capital of Europe.* Rotterdam 2007, p. 37.

56 Philippe Van Parijs: "Why did Brussels become the capital of Europe? Because Belgium starts with letter B." In: Bxl Connect 9 (Summer 2014), p. 8.

57 Cf. Maristella Casciato and Stanislaus von Moos: *Twilight of the Plan. Chandigarh and Brasilia.* Mendrisio 2007.

Berlaymont.[58] In the end, a building that had been shaped by national agendas and private speculations without any comprehensive, long-term vision and required constant modifications, ended up representing the "visual identity" of the supranational institution *par excellence*.

Utopia/Topia

As previously noted, Monnet used to claim that his vision of a European Washington DC had nothing utopian; echoing this belief, Miller wrote that his lake-city was "far from a utopia."[59] That being said, there is a deep connection between the concepts of "plan" and "utopia." In his seminal book *Ideology and Utopia*, Karl Mannheim set up a particularly significant dichotomy, looking at utopia from the perspective of its opposite, which he called "topia," meaning the existing reality: in his reading, topia is any conventional system and utopia is any plan for its replacement.[60] At the center of this opposition is the aforementioned question of finality. Building on Mannheim's theory, Manfredo Tafuri touched on this issue in *Architecture and Utopia*, which, fittingly, was first published in the journal *Contropiano* (which is Italian for "against the plan"). He defined utopia as "the prefiguration of final and universal models."[61] From Tafuri's perspective, the crisis of utopia and the crisis of planning were two faces of the same coin.

This association relates to an ambiguity that has always characterized the definition of utopia, going back to Thomas More's dissertation. The word "topia" derives from the Greek τόπος (place) and can be accompanied by two possible prefixes, which mean different things but are pronounced in the same way: οὐ (no) and εὖ (good).[62] Hence, this concept is built on the ambiguity between the idea of a place that does not exist (ou-topia) and the idea of a good place (eu-topia)—a form of negative dialectics that suggests a certain irreconcilability between possibility and positivity. For example, in his critique of utopian thinking, Theodor Adorno made the case that it is impossible to know "the shape and features of a better society."[63]

From this perspective, the rift between the utopias outlined in Wissembourg, Saarbrücken or Lake Europa and the reality of Brussels is not only a rift between un-

58 European Commission—Visual Identity: https://ec.europa.eu/info/resources-partners/european-commission-visual-identity_en.

59 Jean Monnet: *Memoirs*. London 2015 [1976], p. 369; and James Marshall Miller: *Lake Europa. A New Capital for a United Europe*. New York 1963, p. 88.

60 Cf. Karl Mannheim: *Ideology and Utopia*. London 1936 [1929].

61 Manfredo Tafuri: *Architecture and Utopia*. Cambridge 1976 [1973], p. 53.

62 Cf. Ruth Levitas: *The Concept of Utopia*. Bern 2010.

63 Nina Rismal: *The Ends of Utopian Thinking. Marx, Adorno, Bloch*, PhD thesis, University of Cambridge, 2017; Rismal argues that Adorno, in the context of Critical Theory or, as he called it, *Materialismus*, put forward a form of *Utopieverbot* (ban on utopia).

built plans and unplanned buildings, but also a rift between unbuildable plans and unplannable buildings. In the fragmented, supranational system that has transformed Europe, how could it be possible to build something that aims to transform a totality through a singular, albeit sometimes collaborative, goal-oriented input? On the other hand, what gets built is the result of dynamics that zigzag, move forward without a plan and do not have a finality. As such, they do not threaten anyone and, through small steps and spillovers, they are amenable to be turned into concrete achievements. Over time, these "pack-donkey buildings" spontaneously emerge as the front view of the system.

Yet the utopian dimension is essential, because without the prospect of one day reaching the "promised land," a prospect associated with the idea (some say the myth) of a united Europe, the prosaic, bureaucratic process of European integration would not have started and would not keep going.[64] In this framework, the question raised by Brussels and the other unplanned front views of European integration is one of both method and content: Once the possibility of a single plan is negated *a priori*, how does a process produce architecture?

64 Cf. Peter Burgess: "What's so European about the European Union? Legitimacy between Institution and Identity." In: *European Journal of Social Theory* 5 (2002) pp. 467–481.

Chapter 3
Whatever Happened to Supranational Architecture?

Abstract

The process of European integration is often described in architectural terms, starting with the metaphor of a common European house. This chapter weighs the ubiquitous rhetoric of supranational architecture against the largely unexplored reality of the actual architecture that has been built to house the European institutions. The focus is on the place and time that experienced the largest production of architectural hardware: Brussels between 1958 and 1992. This was the window in which most of the *Quartier Européen* was built, while the institutions did not have a permanent status and therefore struggled to gain agency over the transformations of the city. On one hand, the goal is to question how operating for a new and unique structure of power influenced the production of architecture. On the other hand, this is an opportunity to start discussing how architecture contributed to shaping the European Union.

Europe/European Union

In addressing the theme of this special issue of *Ardeth*, titled *Europe: Architecture, Infrastructure and Territory*, the first step has to be clarification, pertaining to both language and content. The discourse on this topic has constantly been accompanied by an ambiguity, which has generated a multitude of misunderstandings, between two different terms: Europe and the European Union (along with its previous incarnations). This distinction refers to another set of terms that have often been confused: Europeanization and European integration.

In his essay, "What's so European about the European Union?" Peter Burgess has gone to the core of this rift, underlining the tension between "an understanding of Europe as purveyor of a certain kind of cultural identity and the more or less bureaucratic project of European construction undertaken in its name" (Burgess, 2002). Part of the confusion has to do with the fact that these terms are difficult to define. One aspect that certainly sets them apart is their historical breadth. European integration is a recent phenomenon, with a specific start date: it formally began with the signing of the Paris Treaty in 1951, which established the European Coal and Steel Community. In the joint statement issued on that occasion by the foreign ministers of the six founding countries — Belgium, France, Italy, Luxembourg, Netherlands and West Germany — the new community was described as "the first supranational institution" in Europe (Haas, 1958).

That being said, anyone willing to explore the vast literature on European integration will have a hard time finding a clear definition of this phenomenon. The one defining feature on which there is broad consensus is that European integration is a *process*. Historian Desmond Dinan has described it as a "voluntary sharing of national sovereignty in a supranational entity subject to the rule of law" (Dinan, 2006). So, it comes down to a group of states gradually agreeing to a common set of rules and institutions. Not to be confused with the age-old, elusive idea — started as a myth — of Europe.

Even though European integration has taken center stage in a multitude of disciplines, from political science to law and economics, this is not the case when it comes to architecture and urban studies. In the introduction to his seminal book on the identity of European architecture, for example, Vittorio Gregotti prefaces his analysis by saying that it "prescinds completely from the dynamics of the European Union" (Gregotti, 1999). The architectural discourse has often been considered too Eurocentric and too politicized: yet we have mostly ignored the political dynamic that, more than any other, has been transforming the European archipelago over the past seventy years.

Brussels's Hardware

Brussels is the most appropriate place to start exploring how architecture contributed to shaping European integration, not only because it has been the epicenter of the architectural projects for the European Union, but also because, due its particular history and internal power dynamics, it can be read as a microcosm of integration.

In the early 2000s, the European Commission organized a conference titled *Brussels, Capital of Europe* to "discuss the needs and functions of a European capital and how Brussels could best express them" (European Commission, 2001). The core of the event was a debate between Umberto Eco and Rem Koolhaas on how to approach the question of a supranational capital. Eco's argument revolved around the idea of a *soft* capital: "A European capital should deal with soft, not hard, business. So, allow me to smile when I hear that maybe we need to make a monument to give Brussels its character of capital of Europe: an Empire State building, a Coliseum, or something like that — that is hard stuff."

The Dutch architect, on the other hand, was asked by the Commission to present the other side of the argument. For the conference, his team elaborated a presentation titled *Communicating Europe*, exploring ways to effectively represent the

1 Brussels: aerial views of the Quartier Leopold in 1939. Source: Centre Virtuel de la Connaissance sur l'Europe.

2 Brussels: aerial views of the Quartier Leopold in 1999. Source: Centre Virtuel de la Connaissance sur l'Europe.

European Union. This study constituted the basis for the development of the exhibition *The Image of Europe*, which took place in Brussels three years later. The debate revolved around issues of representation — the question of Europe's image — conforming to a tendency to address the European district in Brussels as an immaterial entity. In the same period as the conference, Jean Baudrillard described it as "an abstract place" (Baudrillard, 2002).

However, the transformation of Brussels centered on the production of a massive amount of architectural *hardware*. In the most comprehensive study of this subject, Carola Hein underlined that Brussels was the city with the biggest increase of office space in continental Europe during the second half of the twentieth century (Hein, 2004). According to the Atelier de Recherche et d'Action Urbaines, by the 2000s, the three major institutions alone — European Commission, Parliament and Council — occupied almost two million square meters of office space in the Belgian capital, spread among more than seventy buildings, inhabited by roughly fifty thousand employees (Arau, 2010) (Figs. 1–2).

The opposition "soft capital versus hard capital" framed by the Commission responds to the same logic that informs the dichotomy between the idea of Europe and the reality of the European Union. Overriding any speculation on what a united Europe ought to be or could have been, Brussels is the physical materialization of what the European Union actually is and has been so far. President Trump famously called Brussels a "hellhole" (Buruma, 2016). Steering clear of any value judgements, we shall approach it as a *topia*, as opposed to the utopias (and the dystopias) that are often associated with the integration process.

The Impotent Architect

In addition to its magnitude and the fact that very little attention has been paied to it, the transformation of Brussels has two distinctive characteristics. First, the majority of the aforementioned *hardware* was built over a 34-year period during which the Belgian city was indeed a seat of the European institutions, but only with a provisional status.

Immediately after the signing of the Rome Treaty in 1957, which turned the European Coal and Steel Community into the more ambitious European Economic Community, Brussels emerged as the "executive capital" of the new system, joining Strasbourg and Luxembourg, which had already been identified as the centers of the legislative and judicial powers.

The first group of European officials, roughly three hundred people, moved to Brussels at the beginning of 1958. Notably, this was not the result of a clear plan: on January 1st, when the new institutions of the Community were scheduled to begin operations, the representatives of the member states had not yet found an agreement on a common location and, therefore, decided to start by rotating the meetings in their national capitals. The rotation was based on alphabetical order, so Belgium was first. After the Commission settled in Brussels, however, it would have been very inconvenient to move, and everyone agreed to stay put. In other words, we would not be talking about Brussels if there was another member state that started with letter "A" (Van Parijs, 2014).

That being said, Brussels's provisional status was due to more than this initial contingency. In fact, until the signing of the Maastricht Treaty in 1992, the process of European integration advanced under the assumption that one day all the institutions would be grouped in a single site, a federal capital on the model of Washington DC. For almost forty years, this idea, first outlined by Jean Monnet in the early 1950s, impeded any settlement of the European institutions from being regarded as permanent.

The second defining characteristic of Brussels's expansion is that, until 1992, due to the provisional status of their presence, the European institutions were not allowed to finance and own their buildings. Therefore, they had very little agency over the development of the *Quartier Européen*. At the same time, the host country was barred from building any permanent installation specifically designed for the European institutions (Lenaerts and Vanvoorden, 2008).

A 1978 report of the European Court of Auditors explains the situation in very clear terms: "The budgetary authorities have so far refused to allow the Community institutions to become owners of the properties they inhabit. The argument put forward by the budgetary authorities is political in nature and concerns the lack of any final decision over the official seat of the institutions" (European Court of Auditors, 1978).

As a result, the European institutions had to rent office space in buildings owned and designed by others — an exchange that, by the way, continued to take place well beyond the 1992 turn, because at that point it had become difficult to completely restructure a system that had been solidifying for decades. As highlighted in the report of the Court of Auditors, this situation proved to be extremely costly for the institutions and beneficial for local real-estate companies: a diagram developed by the firm Healey & Baker shows a fivefold increase in the cost of rent in the *Quartier Européen* between the mid-1960s and 1990 (Healey & Baker, 1990).

On the one hand, this condition shines a light on the structural impotence or powerlessness of the European Community as it pertained to the production of architecture throughout more than half of its history. On the other hand, it raises the question of how the massive conglomeration of architecture for the European institutions was produced during that time. Who produced it? And what logic did they follow?

The Berlaymont

The project that kickstarted and focalized the transformation of the Leopold Quarter, the area immediately south-east of Brussels's inner ring road, into a European district was the Berlaymont, the headquarters of the European Commission—an architectural endeavor that spanned almost the entirety of the above-mentioned 34-year-period of provisionality and powerlessness.

The idea of creating a major office building on the site of the Berlaymont monastery was put forward shortly after the first group of *fonctionnaires* moved to Brussels in 1958 (Sterken, 2009). Three entities participated in this endeavor: the Belgian government, represented by its Ministry of Public Works, which owned the site and organized the transfer of the monastery to another location; the Belgian Office of Overseas Social Security, a social security fund designed to deal with international matters (following the dissolution of Belgium's colonial empire), which was brought in by the government to finance the construction of the new Berlaymont; and finally the local real estate company François et Fils, a powerful and very well politically connected company, which promoted the project, pitched the idea to the Commission and oversaw the construction process.

Even though François et Fils had approached the Commission as soon as the first officials arrived, the Belgian government was initially very skeptical about making a major investment for an institution that was in town on a provisional basis and might have left after a short period of time. As noted in a report of the Council of the Brussels Capital Region, the solution was to develop the project on two levels: "Mais par précaution, le programme prévoit que le bâtiment puisse éventuellement abriter un ministère belge, au cas où les institutions européennes ne s'y installeraient pas" (Conseil de la Region de Bruxelles-Capitale, 2003).

When the maquette of the initial project—designed by local architects Lucien de Vestel, Jean Gilson, André and Jean Polak—was shown to the public in 1959, the presentation stated that the building could house *either* a national ministry *or* a European institution "éventuellement prétend-il" (De Beule, 2017).

COMMISSION
DES
COMMUNAUTES EUROPEENNES

Bruxelles, le -7 V 69

IX/C/ 810

Note à l'attention de Monsieur FREDDI
Président de la Commission de contrôle

Ainsi que vous l'avez sans doute appris, le Conseil, dans le cadre du plan de regroupement des institutions européennes à Bruxelles, a décidé que les services de la Commission seraient regroupés dans les complexes Berlaymont et Joyeuse Entrée - Cortenbeeg - Loi, et devraient par conséquent abandonner tous les autres immeubles.

Ceci a donc pour conséquence que l'immeuble Archimède, où la Commission de contrôle est actuellement installée, doit être abandonné.

J'ai donc l'honneur de vous faire connaître qu'il vous est proposé de transférer vos services au 2ème étage du complexe Berlaymont, où 21 bureaux leur ont été réservés, ainsi que les salles d'archives H et I (voir plan ci-annexé).

Je vous saurais gré de bien vouloir me faire connaître quel plan de cloisonnement vous souhaitez voir réaliser.

Je vous signale à ce propos que le nombre de bureaux accordé par le Conseil a conduit la Commission à satisfaire d'autre façon deux obligations traditionnelles :

- d'une part, les services ne pourront plus disposer de salles de réunions internes, mais devront recourir à des salles mises en pool et gérées par la division IX/C/5, à laquelle elles devront être demandées ;

...

Adresse provisoire: 23-27, avenue de la Joyeuse Entrée, Bruxelles 4 – Téléphone 35.00.40-35.01.40 – Adresse télégraphique: «COMEUR Bruxelles» – Télex: «COMEURBRU 21.877»

3 Letter concerning the "plan de cloisonnément" of the Berlaymont, 1969.
Source: European Commission.

Although it had informally expressed its interest in occupying the Berlaymont from the get-go, the European Commission had no say over the design of the building. Suffice it to say that the initial project did not include appropriate facilities for translators, which are obviously essential to the functioning of a supranational institution.

The architects, who had been single-handedly selected by the Belgian Ministry of Public Works (without a competition), were asked to design the interiors according to an open-plan layout, which aligned with the way work was organized and carried out in most Belgian government buildings. This layout, however, conflicted with the way the Commission operated. In 1968, when the building was completed and the parties started to negotiate the lease, this issue came to the fore in a major way: the compromise came in the form of a sizeable discount on the rent.

Before the first *fonctionnaire* could start working in the Berlaymont, however, the entire interior had to be restructured. The correspondence between the Président de la Commission de Contrôle, the Directeur Général du Personnel et de l'Administration and the Chef de la Division Immeubles-Matériel-Service Intérieur during that time speaks to the tension that came with this process (European Commission, 1969).

One of the key issues had to do with the fact that multiple departments, especially those that dealt with economic matters, needed to operate with a high degree of "autonomie" and therefore could not be placed in an open space where others could physically interfere with their activities. The solution was to implement a comprehensive "plan de cloisonnement," which turned the initial open layout into a maze of enclosed spaces, characterized by long, dark corridors, leaving many offices without windows (Fig. 3).

UNESCO and Nestlé

The architectural project for the "centre administratif Europe" was assigned by the Belgian Ministry of Public Works to a group of local architects: Lucien de Vestel, Jean Gilson, André Polak, Jean Polak and Joris Schmidt. Again, there was no competition. The lead architect, Lucien de Vestel, was a modernist, mostly known for its design of the Belgian pavilion at the Paris Colonial Exposition in 1931. Andrè and Jean Polak were involved in the design of the Atomium, the centrepiece of Brussels's 1958 Expo. As noted by Sven Streken and Dennis Pohl, "no statement remains by the architects of the Berlaymont concerning their design intentions" but "they seem to have deduced the form and expression of the building from functional and structural considerations." The design concept entailed a cruciform shape with four wings of unequal size, projecting from a central, concrete core (Fig. 4). The wings were suspended from cantilevered beams on the penultimate floor, anchored to the core. The suspension was meant to provide a sense of lightness and openness on the ground floor. The reception in the public discourse was all about the innovative nature of this concrete and steel system, which was presented as a feat of engineering.

Most of the sources on this project mention that the X-shaped layout of the Berlaymont was directly inspired by the UNESCO building in Paris, which had been realized between 1955 and 1958, under the direction of Marcel Breuer, Pier Luigi Nervi and Bernard Zehrfuss. We know that a delegation of European officials went to visit this building in 1961. In an interview with Carola Hein, however, Jean Polak pointed to another model: the Nestlé headquarters in Vevey, Switzerland, designed by Jean Tschumi. This project started in 1956 and was completed in 1960. This back and forth has to do with the fact that, from a formal as well as structural point of view, the headquarters of the European Commission in Brussels, UNESCO in Paris and Nestlé in Vevey were remarkably similar.

The case of UNESCO is particularly relevant because, as an international organization, it raised some of the same questions as the European Commission with regards to the relation with national authorities. The land on which the UNESCO headquarters are built is property of the French state. In 1952, the French Foreign Ministry arranged a lease for a term of 99 years with UNESCO. The lease was accompanied by a "headquarters agreement" which defined the privileges and immunities of UNESCO. The French Parliament was called to approve the lease and authorize the government to ratify the agreement. The main precedent was the United Nations building in New York City, of which UNESCO is a specialized agency. In that case, the land was donated to the UN in 1946 by the Rockefeller family, who owned the site in Manhattan. Thereafter, the UN signed a treaty with the US government, which established the site as an "extraterritorial" zone, under the sole administration of the UN. These agreements allowed both the UN and UNESCO to take control of their site and drive their respective architectural projects. In the case of UNESCO, for example, the institution appointed in 1951 a panel of advisors, presided by Walter Gropius, which included Ernesto Nathan Rogers, Lucio Costa, Sven Markelius and Eero Saarinen. After a few months Le Corbusier joined the group, on the heels of his involvement in the UN project in New York.

Concurrently, UNESCO commissioned a proposal to a local architect, Eugene Beaudouin. So, it was not a competition, but rather a direct appointment. The task of the advisory panel was to evaluate such a proposal, which was quickly deemed inadequate. In 1952, therefore, UNESCO made a second appointment to a team composed of Breuer, Nervi and Zehrfuss. This triumvirate took the project forward, with the support of the advisory panel. The main point is that UNESCO oversaw these decisions and, recognizing the importance of the project, moved to take on board a selection of some of the most influential figures in the field of architecture at the time. As in the case of the UN headquarters in New York, there was also a clear intention to embrace modern architecture and, more specifically, the international style as the ideal expression for a true international organization.

The comparison between the headquarters of UNESCO, Nestlé and the European Commission, built one after the other in rapid succession between the mid-1950s and the mid-1960s, is interesting on multiple levels. While the three buildings look very similar, the processes behind these cases reveal profound differences, pertaining to the specificity of the institutions that produced or inhabited these spaces. This is an opportunity to put a finger on the difference between international, multinational and supranational organizations. UNESCO is an international body: a space where representatives of national institutions come together, negotiate and cooperate. The project for the Paris headquarters responds to the same logic: the architects were a selection of key figures from powerful nations or nations that, in a way, mattered in the field of architecture. The way the designers and the members of the advisory panels worked together in this project matched the intergovernmental *modus operandi* of the institution.

The Nestlé building in Switzerland was partly inspired by the UNESCO project. In this case, we have a multinational corporation mirroring the architecture of an international organization. From an institutional standpoint, the difference is that the former branches out from a center (more often than not, in Switzerland) and governs processes in a multitude of countries, while the latter is a meeting place, where governments of different countries come together to make deals. The European Commission is neither of these things. The concept of supra-nationalization entails a rescaling of the member states, which agree to give away a significant part of their sovereign power to an entity operating above them. This is drastically more complex than creating a space, as in the case of UNESCO or the UN, where member states sit around a table and negotiate, on the basis of their national interest. The development of the Berlaymont speaks to this difficulty: the process was certainly not run according to supranational logic.

From Poison to Symbol

After a long series of further modifications, shortly before Brussels was recognized as a permanent seat of the European institutions, the perspective changed again in 1990, when vast quantities of asbestos were detected in the Berlaymont. Notably, a significant percentage of the 1400 tons of poisonous materials found in the building was embedded in the partitions that had been added over the years to create separate offices.

The building could not be demolished because its foundations anchored the local road and metro network, so the parties decided to embark on a long and expensive renovation process. The Belgian government did not have the resources to pay for this project, so it teamed up with a number of private investors, mostly banks and financial institutions (Citibank, CGER, BACOB, among others), which set up a company called *Berlaymont 2000* in order to fund and manage the renovation. In exchange for this investment, the company obtained from the government a long lease on the building, which was then sublet to the European Commission at a higher price.

When the asbestos crisis came up, several European officials proposed to take this opportunity to leave a building that had been designed for something else and never fit. However, the local authorities argued that the Berlaymont had become a "symbol" of the European presence in Brussels and therefore needed to be preserved (Shore, 2000).

By the same token, when the Commission decided to create a logo in the mid-2000s, the selected design centered on the silhouette of the Berlaymont (European Commission, 2017). In the end, a building that had been shaped by national agendas and private speculations, required constant modification and threatened the health of its inhabitants, ended up representing the "visual identity" of the supranational institution *par excellence.*

Bruxellisation

As evidenced by the case of the Berlaymont, the private sector played a key role in the transformation of Brussels. As noted by Alex Papadopoulos, Brussels is an atypical Western European capital because it was never subject to a comprehensive urban regulatory regime and most of its changes were based on private financing, following models of development that are often found in the United States (Padadopoulos, 1996).

Four years after the arrival of the European institutions, in 1962, Belgium made its first attempt at introducing a national regulation and passed the *Loi Organique de l'Aménagement du Territoire et de l'Urbanisme.* This regulatory regime characterized all the period during which Brussels acted as a provisional seat of the European institutions, because it remained in force until 1991, when it was replaced by the *Ordonnance Organique de la Planification et de l'Urbanisme.* The "organic law" is well-known among planners because, rather than trying to guide the transformations of the city, it established a *laissez-faire* approach. The result was a process known as Bruxellisation — a term commonly used to indicate the demolition of large sections of the historic fabric of the city and the haphazard construction of high-rise office buildings (Kapplinger, 1993).

Part of the problem was that Belgium, much like the European Union, is a federal system and, over the years, had to find ways to bring together a trilingual, tricultural population: any strict regulation imposed by the national government was unlikely to be easily accepted by these diverse communities, especially in the 1960s, a period of harsh confrontation between the Flemish and Walloon regions.

Parliament in Disguise

Nowhere is the agency of private developers on the production of architecture for the European institutions clearer than in the case of the Spinelli building, the headquarters of the European Parliament in Brussels. If the vicissitudes of the Berlaymont speak mostly to the tensions associated with the early phases of the period under consideration, the Spinelli building relates to the other end of our timeline and shines a light on the turning point of 1992. In fact, the development of the hemicycle began in the mid-1980s, and the complex was inaugurated in 1995.

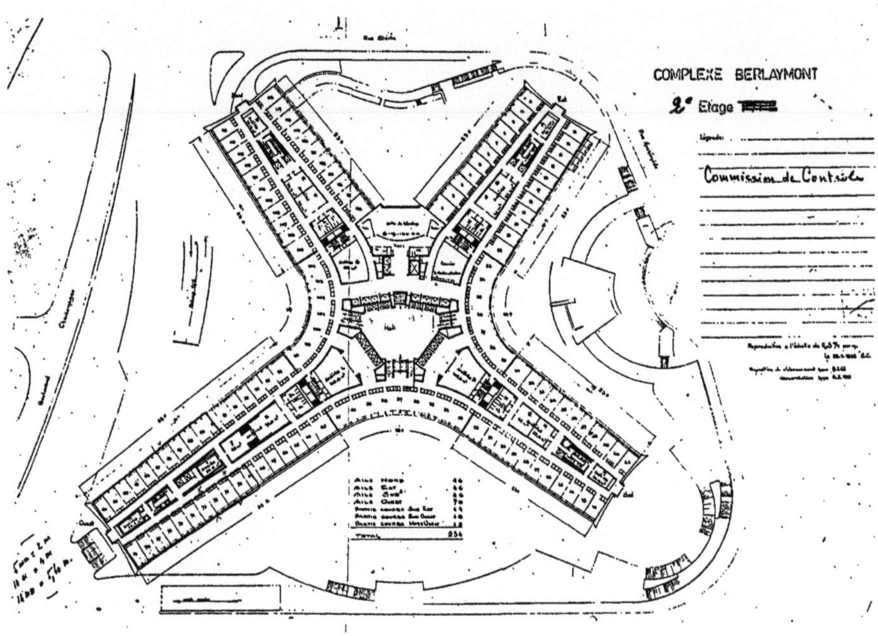

4 Plan of the Berlaymont after the reorganization of the interiors, 1969.
Source: European Commission.

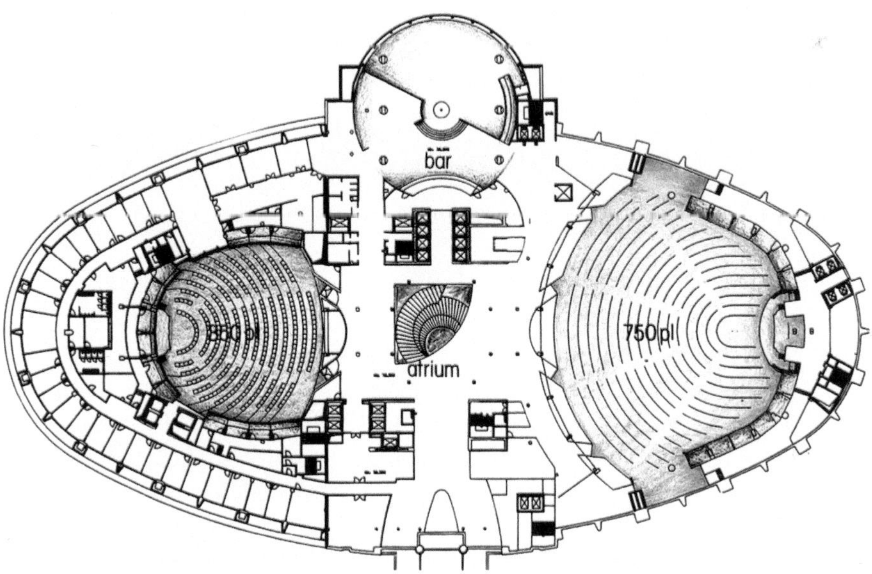

5 Plan of the “Centre International de Conférences,” 1988.
Source: Michel Boucquillon.

As previously noted, the informal organizational structure of the EU indicated that the legislative branch was to be in Strasbourg: the parliamentary assembly had been meeting in the French city since the birth of the European Coal and Steel Community. However, as more and more activities progressively coalesced in Brussels over the years, in the 1980s the European Parliament started to lobby in order to have a seat near the executive branch.

The idea of moving to Brussels obviously clashed with the standpoint of the French government, which put its foot down to protect the Strasbourg headquarters. A 1987 Le Monde article titled *Bataille pour un Hémicyle* speaks to the level of tension that underlaid this discussion (Fralon, 1987). So how did the Parliament get around this obstacle?

A report of the Council of the Brussels Capital Region clearly states that, in 1988, "l'Etat belge a voulu construire le siège du Parlement sans le dire officiellement; l'Etat belge trouve un groupement d'investisseurs, ou inversement d'ailleurs, et le groupement construit pour le compte officieux du Parlement et de l'Etat belge" (Conseil de la Region de Bruxelles-Capitale, 1991). This and many other documents point to the fact that Brussels's seat of the European Parliament was built *in disguise* (Lamant, 2018).

There was an informal agreement with the European institutions from the beginning but, as noted in another report of the Council, "la construction d'un hémicycle ont été formellement négociées avec les autorités européennes" (Conseil de la Region de Bruxelles-Capitale, 2003). The solution was to use a false name: instead of saying they were building a hemicycle for the European Parliament, the developers called it "Centre Internationale de Conférence," often shortened to the acronym "CIC" (Fig. 6).

The whole operation was promoted by a group of investors called *Societé Espace Leopold*, led by two Belgian banks: Société Générale de Belgique and BACOB, which was involved in the renovation of the Berlaymont too. These financial institutions owned the site of the Leopold brewery, less than a mile away from the Berlaymont. In June 1987, they signed an agreement with the government of the Brussels Capital Region and, in July 1987, obtained a building permit to demolish the existing structure of the brewery and build an "International Conference Centre" on the site (Papadopoulos, 1996).

The way in which the design was selected and developed was in line with the overall *ethos* of this project. The consortium of banks and investors teamed up with a consortium of Belgian architects, which called themselves *Association des Architectes du Centre Internationale de Conférence*. The architectural firms that composed this association, however, were not interested in elaborating a design and, instead, organized an informal competition, aiming to find a proposal that was ready to be executed. The design ended up being produced by Michel Boucquillon, a 26-year-old, recently graduated, local architect, who was selected as the winner of this unusual contest (Fig. 5).

From an institutional point of view, the informal agreement between the developers and the European authorities was eventually legitimized by the 1992 decision regarding the status of the headquarters, which stated that Strasbourg would re-

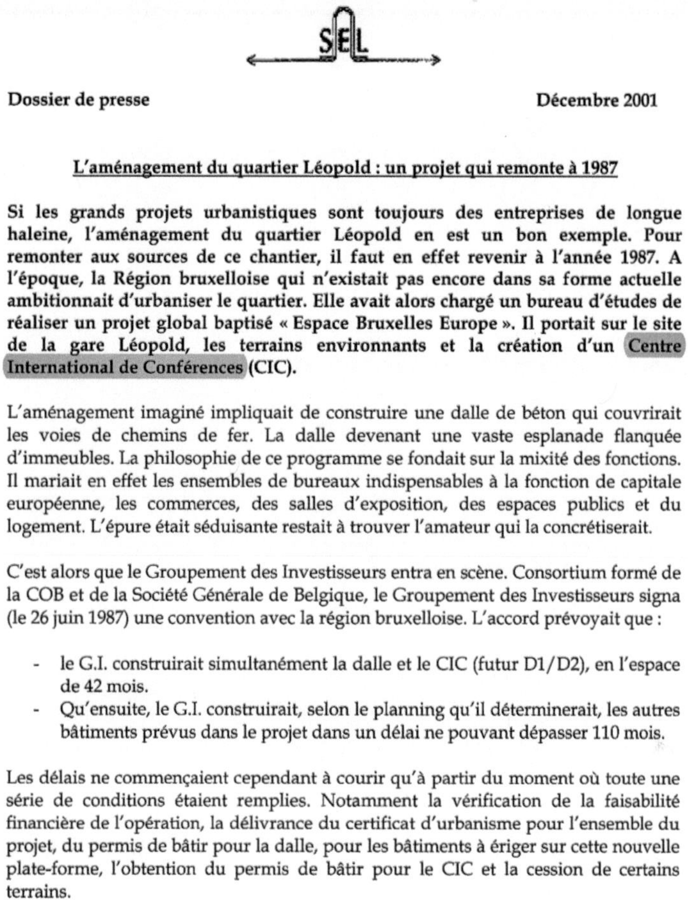

Dossier de presse **Décembre 2001**

L'aménagement du quartier Léopold : un projet qui remonte à 1987

Si les grands projets urbanistiques sont toujours des entreprises de longue haleine, l'aménagement du quartier Léopold en est un bon exemple. Pour remonter aux sources de ce chantier, il faut en effet revenir à l'année 1987. A l'époque, la Région bruxelloise qui n'existait pas encore dans sa forme actuelle ambitionnait d'urbaniser le quartier. Elle avait alors chargé un bureau d'études de réaliser un projet global baptisé « Espace Bruxelles Europe ». Il portait sur le site de la gare Léopold, les terrains environnants et la création d'un Centre International de Conférences (CIC).

L'aménagement imaginé impliquait de construire une dalle de béton qui couvrirait les voies de chemins de fer. La dalle devenant une vaste esplanade flanquée d'immeubles. La philosophie de ce programme se fondait sur la mixité des fonctions. Il mariait en effet les ensembles de bureaux indispensables à la fonction de capitale européenne, les commerces, des salles d'exposition, des espaces publics et du logement. L'épure était séduisante restait à trouver l'amateur qui la concrétiserait.

C'est alors que le Groupement des Investisseurs entra en scène. Consortium formé de la COB et de la Société Générale de Belgique, le Groupement des Investisseurs signa (le 26 juin 1987) une convention avec la région bruxelloise. L'accord prévoyait que :

- le G.I. construirait simultanément la dalle et le CIC (futur D1/D2), en l'espace de 42 mois.
- Qu'ensuite, le G.I. construirait, selon le planning qu'il déterminerait, les autres bâtiments prévus dans le projet dans un délai ne pouvant dépasser 110 mois.

Les délais ne commençaient cependant à courir qu'à partir du moment où toute une série de conditions étaient remplies. Notamment la vérification de la faisabilité financière de l'opération, la délivrance du certificat d'urbanisme pour l'ensemble du projet, du permis de bâtir pour la dalle, pour les bâtiments à ériger sur cette nouvelle plate-forme, l'obtention du permis de bâtir pour le CIC et la cession de certains terrains.

6 Report of the developers of the "Centre International de Conférences," 2001.
Source: Société Espace Léopold.

main the primary seat of the Parliament and hold its monthly plenary sessions, but all the additional sessions, as well as the meetings of the parliamentary committees, could take place in Brussels. Because of this arrangement, as soon as the "Centre Internationale de Conférence" was completed in 1995, the Parliament rented it and started to use the new hemicycle, ironically renaming it after Altiero Spinelli, whose idea of European integration had very little to do with this construction method.

Whatever Happened to Supranational Architecture?

Given its complexity, multiple theories have been developed over the years to interpret and explain how the process of European integration works (Wiener and Diez, 2004). Architectural case studies such as the Berlaymont and the Spinelli building, however, provide the unique opportunity to anchor these reflections to tangible objects. For example, Lennaert Van Heumen and Mechthild Roos's theory of "informal integration" or Jack Hayward's theory of "integration by stealth" can be juxtaposed to the unofficial, behind-the-scenes, hidden practices that made these buildings possible (Van Heumen and Roos, 2019; Hayward, 1996). It is hard to find a clearer example of informal, stealthy architecture than the "Centre Internationale de Conférence."

Nonetheless, architecture has entered the discourse on European integration only on a metaphorical level. In one of the rare studies of this subject, Paul Chilton has highlighted the role of the metaphor of the "common European house" in the integration process (Chilton, 1993). But there are many other examples: the publications on the "institutional architecture" of the European Union are too many to count. By the same token, Jean Monnet, Robert Schuman and the other founding fathers are constantly referred to as the *architects* of European integration.

Once we step away from this metaphorical dimension and start to look at the actual institutional architecture of the European Union — the one made of concrete, steel, glass (and occasionally asbestos) — we gain a different perspective. As in the cases of the buildings of the Commission and the Parliament, the two institutions that, more than any other, represent the transition from a system of divided nation states to one of integrated member states, the rhetoric of a supranational institutional architecture clashes with the reality of a process of architectural production that responds primarily to local, regional, national and at most intergovernmental dynamics, with a strong influence of the private sector.

On the one hand, architecture serves as a testing ground. While most of the research on European integration deals with immaterial objects, architecture provides concrete case studies that can help us decipher how the European Union works. Being careful not to generalize and overreach, one may argue that exploring how these buildings are produced illuminates how things take form in this integrated system and how the European Union operates as a *builder* in other areas as well.

On the other hand, the way the system is structured seems to challenge the very possibility of architecture. As underlined by Joschka Fischer in his influential speech *Thoughts on the Finality of European Integration*, European integration operates as "a gradual process with no blueprint" (Fischer, 2000). Since its inception, this has been the *modus operandi*: as early as 1950, the Schuman Declaration clearly stated that "Europe

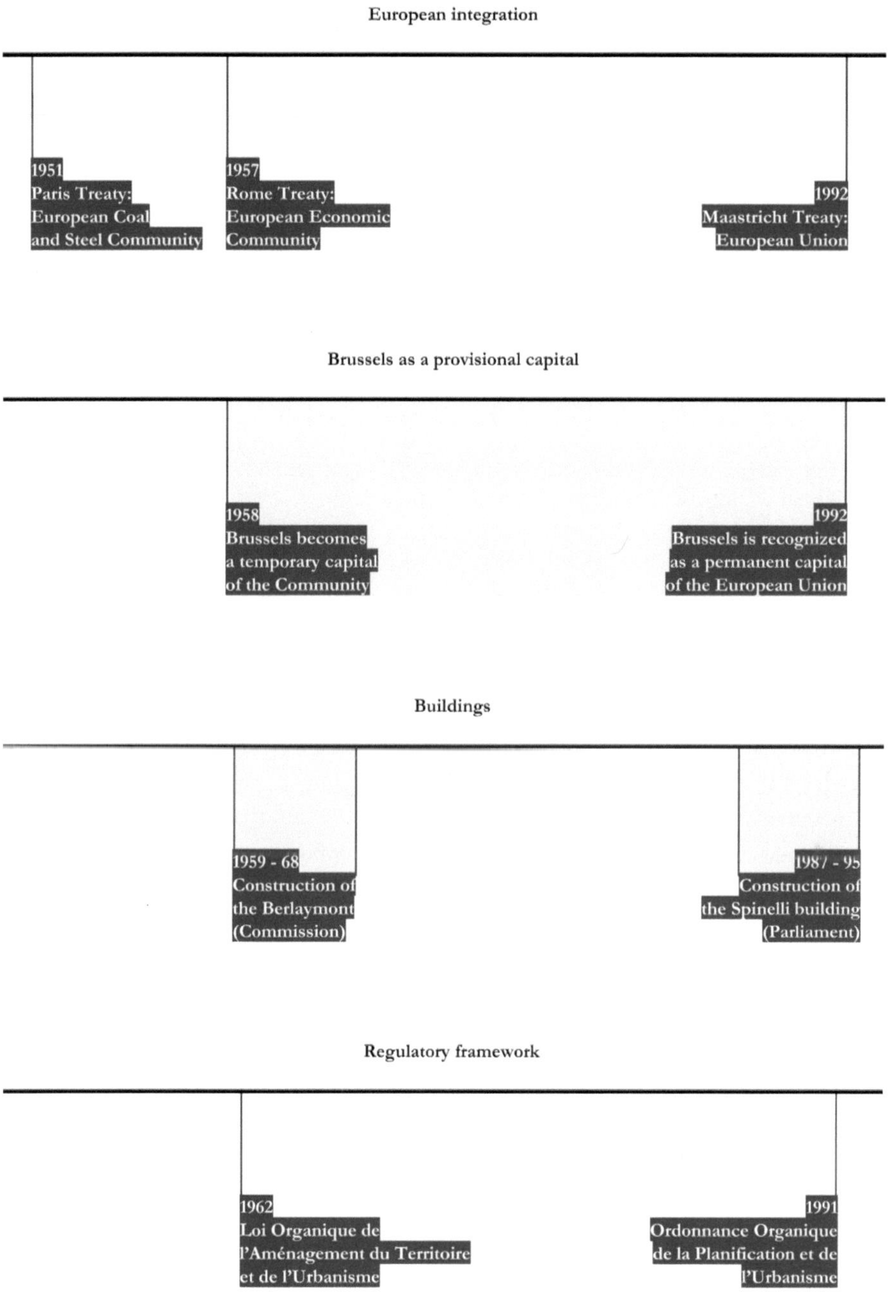

7 Timeline.
Source: Author.

will not be made all at once, or according to a single, general plan; it will be built through concrete achievements" (Krijtenburg, 2012).

We are used to thinking that the presence of a blueprint, a plan or some kind of outline regarding how things need to unfold is the *conditio sine qua non* for the production of architecture. In our field, every "concrete achievement" is preceded by plans, elevations, sections. From this point of view, European integration poses an existential question: once the possibility of a blueprint is negated *a priori*, how does a process produce architecture?

References

Arau: Atelier de Recherche et d'Action Urbaines (2010), *Petite Chronique du Ghetto Européen à Son Apogee*, Brussels, Arau.

Baudrillard, J. (2002), *Europe, Globalization and the Destiny of Culture*, "European Journal of Social Theory," vol. 5, n. 4, pp. 521–530.

Burgess, P. (2002), *What's so European about the European Union? Legitimacy between Institution and Identity*, "European Journal of Social Theory," vol. 5, n. 4, pp. 465–479.

Buruma, I. (2016), *In the Capital of Europe*, "The New York Review of Books," April 7th.

Chilton, P. (1993), *Metaphor in Political Discourse: The Case of the Common European House*, "Discourse & Society," vol. 4, n. 1, pp. 7–31.

Conseil de la Region de Bruxelles-Capitale (1991), *Proposition de resolution relative au role de Bruxelles dans l'accueil des Institutions Europeennes* [Online]. Available at: https://www.moniteur.be [Accessed 15 November 2020].

Conseil de la Region de Bruxelles-Capitale (2003), *Proposition de resolution concernant l'implantation des Institutions Européennes à Bruxelles* [Online]. Available at: https://www.moniteur.be [Accessed 15 November 2020].

De Beule, M. (ed.) (2017), *Bruxelles, Histoire de Planifier: Urbanisme aux 19e et 20e Siècles*, Brussels, Mardaga.

Dinan, D. (ed.) (2006), *Origins and Evolution of the European Union*, Oxford, Oxford University Press.

European Commission (1969), *Correspondence regarding the organization of office space in the Berlaymont* [Online]. Available at: https://ec.europa.eu/historical_archives [Accessed 15 November 2020].

European Commission (2001), *Brussels, Capital of Europe* [Online]. Available at: https://ec.europa.eu/historical_archives [Accessed 15 November 2020].

European Commission (2017), *Visual Identity Manual* [Online]. Available at: https://ec.europa.eu/historical_archives [Accessed 15 November 2020].

European Court of Auditors (1978), *Note for the attention of the members of the Court of Auditors concerning the lease for a new building* [Online]. Available at: https://archives.eui.eu [Accessed 15 November 2020].

Fischer, J. (2000), *Thoughts on the Finality of European Integration* [Online]. Available at: https://ec.europa.eu/historical_archives [Accessed 15 November 2020].

Fralon, J. (1987), *Bataille pour un Hémicyle*, "Le Monde," July 2nd.

Gregotti, V. (1999), *L'Identità dell'Architettura Europea e la Sua Crisi*, Turin, Einaudi.

Haas, E. (1958), *The Uniting of Europe*, Stanford, Stanford University Press.

Hayward, J. (ed.) (1996), *Elitism, Populism and European Politics*, Oxford, Clarendon Press.

Healey & Baker (1990), *Growth of Rental Properties at the Quartier Européen*, London, Healey & Baker.

Hein, C. (2004), *The Capital of Europe: Architecture and Urban Planning for the European Union*, Wesport, Praeger.

Kapplinger, C. (1993), *Façadisme et Bruxellisation*, "Bauwelt," vol. 84, n. 40, pp. 2166–2175.

Krijtenburg, M. (2012), *Schuman's Europe*, Leiden, Leiden University Press.

Lamant, L. (2018), *Bruxelles Chantiers: Une Critique Architectural de l'Europe*, Montreal, Lux.

Lenaerts, K. and Vanvoorden, K. (2008), *The Legal Status of Brussels as European Capital*, in De Groof, R. (ed.), *Brussels and Europe*, Brussels, Academic and Scientific Publishers.

Papadopoulos, A. (1996), *Urban Regimes and Strategies: Building Europe's Central Executive District in Brussels*, Chicago, University of Chicago Press.

Shore, C. (2000), *Building Europe: The Cultural Politics of European Integration*, London, Routledge.

Sterken, S. (2009), *Le Berlaymont et la Transformation du Quartier Leopold*, "Journées du Patrimoine Région de Bruxelles-Capitale," n. 15, pp. 102–117.

Van Heumen, L. and Roos, M. (eds.) (2019), *The Informal Construction of Europe*, London, Routledge.

Van Parijs, P. (2014), *Why did Brussels become the capital of Europe? Because Belgium starts with the letter B*, "The Brussels Times," September 7th.

Wiener, A. and Diez, T. (eds.) (2004), *European Integration Theory*, Oxford, Oxford University Press.

Chapter 4
Building the European Central Bank

Abstract

The building of the European Central Bank (ECB) in Frankfurt am Main is the result of a complex process, initiated twenty years ago, that intersected and amplified a set of issues concerning the relationship between architecture and power at the turn of the millennium. On the one hand, from the initial competition, launched in 2002, to the inauguration of the tower designed by Coop Himmelb(l)au, this case highlights the reluctance, on the part of the institution, to use architecture to project power and showcase its mission. This hesitancy relates to the ECB's particular status as a supranational institution, operating between multiple national identities. While assuming an increasingly political role, the bank tried to present itself as a neutral, technical body, responding to a model of depoliticized governance. All that mattered was what the institution did, not what it was. This functionalist outlook, on the other hand, aligned with a contemporaneous shift in architectural practice and thought. The traditional concern with representation was challenged by an evolving notion of materialism, which set aside questions of meaning in favor of questions of performance. All that mattered was what buildings did. From this perspective, the performance of the technical infrastructure was believed to be the primary source of meaning, for both the institution and the architecture that housed it. The unfolding of the ECB project, however, revealed the limitations of such approaches. Given the importance of the bank within the governance of the European Union during a time of economic crisis, the building site became the stage for multiple symbolic rituals and forced a difficult reflection on the image of the European community. Despite the efforts to blend in and neutralize architecture, as in the case of the euro banknotes, the building process pushed the ECB to address its unique political dimension, beyond reductive notions of technical efficiency.

Utility established as meaning generates meaninglessness.
Hannah Arendt

From Maastricht to Frankfurt

In November 2002, the European Central Bank (ECB) launched a major competition for the 'planning and design' of its new premises in Frankfurt (ECB 2002: 2). Although the process of European integration had started some fifty years earlier and multiple institutions had been built during that time, the ECB project came in a period of profound transformation and opened the door for a reframing of the relationship between architecture and supranational power. The watershed moment was the signing of the Maastricht Treaty in 1992, which inaugurated 'a new stage' in the integration process, merging the previous European communities into the European Union (EU) and laying the groundwork for the introduction of a common currency (Dinan 2006). One of the reforms coming out of Maastricht concerned the rules of engagement with architecture and the city. Up to that point, no definitive decision had been taken regarding the location of European institutions, which therefore did not have the power to design, build, and own their premises (Hein 2004).

The European Commission, the first institutional experiment in supranational authority par excellence, is a prime example. It was set up in Brussels in the late 1950s simply because Belgium preceded the other member states in alphabetical order. The initial plan was to rotate its seat between all the national capitals — a complex logistical challenge that was immediately dismissed. In the end, the Commission never left Brussels. But, at the same time, Brussels would not be officially recognized as the permanent seat of the Commission until the 1990s, more than thirty years later. The responsibility to construct a home for this institution fell on national and local actors, as the Commission did not have the legal authority to produce its own architecture (Fabbrini 2021a).

The development of the Berlaymont, the office building that serves as the headquarters of the Commission, was carried out by the Belgian government, in collaboration with local real-estate developers. As it was unclear whether the Commission would remain in Brussels, the Berlaymont was initially designed to house a Belgian ministry: the local authorities did not want to make a large investment for a European institution that might leave after a few months. The result was a building that never fit the modus operandi of the Commission, as evidenced by the many attempts to adapt and transform a space that was not conducive to a supranational operation (Sterken 2015).

The case of the European Parliament is even more intricate (Lamant 2018). Its Brussels headquarters were famously developed in secret because the French government opposed moving the institution away from its initial seat, in Strasbourg. For the entire development process, the massive complex that came to house the Parliament in the *quartier européen* was camouflaged as an 'international congress center'.

Whatever It Takes

After Maastricht, the monetary integration project was placed in the hands of a new institution, which was initially called the European Monetary Institute (EMI) and which, in 1998, morphed into the ECB. Well before the bank started operating, the heads of state and government of the EU Council had already decided that its permanent seat would be in Frankfurt, the financial center of the continent. This allowed the new institution to actively address, from the onset, the question of its physical presence in the city. Although the EMI initially rented an existing high-rise (which came to be known as the Eurotower) in the financial district, the plan was to build a new home, specifically designed for its purposes.

Following a 'feasibility study' that considered and evaluated 35 local sites, the ECB eventually purchased the site of the Grossmarkthalle, the old market hall in the Ostend district, from the City of Frankfurt (ECB 2020). The acquisition was preceded by the so-called headquarters agreement between the ECB and the German federal government, which underlined the 'independence' of the institution and the 'inviolability' of its premises (ECB 1998). When the first euro banknotes and coins began to circulate in early 2002, the bank had already laid the groundwork for a design competition for the new site.

In addition to having the power to drive this architectural project—a power that the Commission and the other European institutions did not have at the time of their placement—the ECB is particularly relevant because it oversees monetary integration, the area in which the process of supranationalization has gone the furthest. The introduction of the euro represents the most significant 'deepening' of the European community since its inception (Alesina and Giavazzi 2020). Howarth and Loedel (2005: xi) argue that 'the ECB has become the most important institutional creation in Europe since the institutionalization of the nation state in the seventeenth century; it is the ECB that perhaps best defines the relinquishing of state sovereignty to an institution with powerful supranational mechanisms of decision-making and enforcement'.

If the degree of supranationalization can be measured by the level of autonomy from, and power over, national bodies, the ECB is arguably the most advanced European institution in this respect. As noted by Heisenberg and Richmond (2002), the ECB is not subject to oversight by member state governments, in the manner of the European Commission, which can be overruled by the Council of Ministers, and has greater legal authority than the European Parliament, as it can make legally binding regulations and decisions. It also differs from the European Court of Justice, which has a collaborative relationship with the national courts. The national central banks have in turn become agents of the ECB. They receive directions from Frankfurt, not interpretations that they then apply themselves. Naturally, they also had to give up their gold reserves, which are now owned by the ECB. Furthermore, such authority is not limited to the public sector: with the introduction of the Single Supervisory Mechanism, the ECB has also become the ‘direct supervisor’ of all the large private banks in the eurozone, which amount to more than 80 % of the total banking assets in the EU (Wiggins, Wedow, and Metrick 2019).

Monetary policy was so important that the power and influence of the ECB quickly extended from maintaining price stability in the eurozone, which is the stated task of the institution, to becoming a key actor in its political governance. During the debt crisis of 2008–2009, just when construction of its new headquarters in Frankfurt began, the ECB became, one could argue, the helmsman of the European ship (Athanassiou 2018). During one of the most challenging economic storms in the history of the EU, the president of the ECB said that he was ready to do whatever it took to keep the ship afloat — a declaration of supranational power that no other European institution was ever able to make. Designing the ECB headquarters during those turbulent times was therefore a unique opportunity to help shape the institution that, more than any other, had come to exert power in the complex space of the supranational. It was also the first supranational institution that could truly explore its architectural dimension.

Hyperbolic Form

In September 1994, as the European Monetary Institute had just begun its operations in the Eurotower, the Deutsches Architekturmuseum held an exhibition called *The Bank: Three Architectural Concepts for the Future.* Three renowned firms — David Chipperfield Architects, Eduardo Souto de Moura, and Herzog & de Meuron — were invited to reflect on this typology and imagine ’a fictive project, with a fictive client, a fictive programme and without a fixed location’. The question was, ‘how will the Bank of the Future look?’. Surprisingly, no one mentioned that a new type of bank had just come to Frankfurt. Instead, the focus was on a hypothetical, generic bank branch that could exist in any European city. The ethos of the exhibition was clearly expressed by Herzog & de Meuron, who made the case that the bank of the future ‘will look the way the bank has always looked like and give us the same impression the bank has always given us: a stable, firmly rooted, unmistakable structure, which is immediately recognisable as The Bank in any urban context, despite the plethora of symbols, signs and billboards’ (Chipperfield et al. 1994, cited on Herzog & de Meuron 1994 (website)). Their model consisted of a large, hermetic, cubic volume, oddly reminiscent of Scrooge McDuck’s money bin.

In just a few years, the ECB competition created several layers of complexity in this conversation. Now the problem was more specific and layered (Fig. 1). Jakob + MacFarlane, one of the 71 firms that participated in the competition, framed the question in these terms: ’how could the Central Bank of Europe be represented architecturally?’ (ECB 2003a: 63). Both the institution and the architects were navigating uncharted waters. The need for a change in approach was underlined most directly by

1 Cover of the ECB competition brief, November 2002.
Source: European Central Bank.

OMA, another of the firms in the competition: 'Conceiving a building for the European Central Bank is like flying blind, venturing into a domain with no clear references. So far, the question of a European style or iconography to accommodate Europe's increasing integration has the usual habitat of business: a high-rise tower clad in beige marble with brown mirror glass windows. Besides the building's name *Eurotower*, no effort has been made to present the bank as one of the symbols of a unified Europe' (ECB 2003a: 33).

From the launch of the competition in 2002 to the inauguration of the building in 2015, however, the opportunities and challenges presented by this unique case were constantly understated. The competition brief set the tone immediately. Other than generically acknowledging that the design proposals would constitute 'inspiring contributions to the building of a unified Europe', the organizers of the competition did not highlight any of the political dynamics behind this endeavor (ECB 2002: 3).

According to the brief, one of the most important objectives was the integration and preservation of the Grossmarkthalle. This effort went so far as to remove, clean

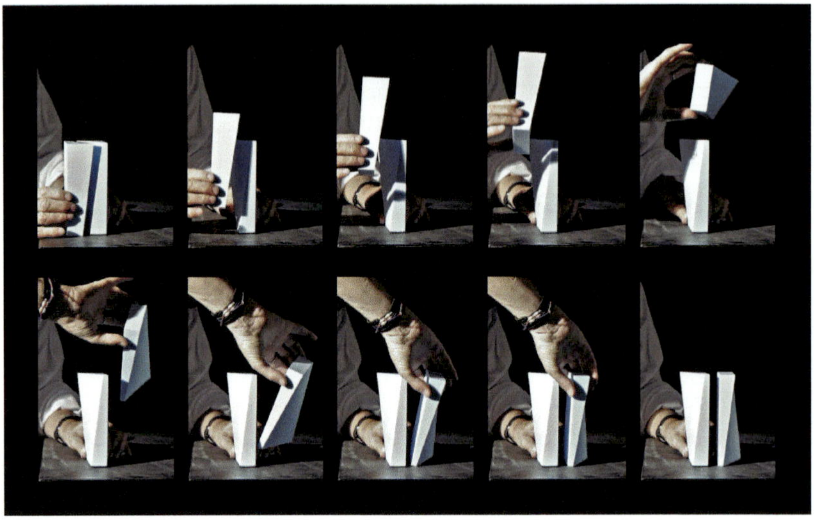

2 Coop Himmelb(l)au illustrates the "hyperboloid cut" of the ECB project, 2004.
Source: Coop Himmelb(l)au.

and reposition the bricks of the existing building. The other major requirement centered on sustainability and energy efficiency (ECB 2002). Coop Himmelb(l)au's winning project focused heavily on this issue, proposing a new type of envelope, called 'shield hybrid façade', which, through a variety of advanced technologies, promised a high degree of climate control in the office space (ECB 2020).

In addition to highlighting this technological apparatus, Coop Himmelb(l)au argued that the project revolved around a decisive formal gesture (Fig. 2): 'The design concept of the ECB is to vertically divide a monolithic block through a hyperboloid cut, wedge it apart, twist it and fill the newly created intermediary space with a glass atrium' (Coop Himmelb(l)au n. d.). The result was a 'twisted double tower' that, from the architect's perspective, responded to the ECB's 'request to create a unique, iconic building as a symbol for the European Union'. Ironically, six years later, a similar concept was submitted to the competition for the new headquarters of the Central Bank of Azerbaijan, which Coop Himmelb(l)au also won.

It was a design concept that aligned with the trend of the time, including presenting the cutting sequence through photos of little blue foam models. But the way this concept engaged with the specificity of the institution was unexplained. Even if we attempt to read the 'hyperboloid cut' in a metaphorical way, which is not the way it was supposed to be read, it is difficult to find a connection with the ECB. The formal operation of dividing a monolith into two towers obviously clashes with the logic of European integration, which implies bringing together and uniting separate entities.

Updating the Politics of Architecture

In 2008, as the financial crisis was exploding and the ECB project was getting off the ground, Alejandro Zaera-Polo published 'The Politics of the Envelope', which gave voice to a changing understanding of the relationship between architecture and politics: 'Architects' traditional role as visionaries (and ideologists) has become redundant as the sheer speed of change overtakes their capacity to represent politics ideologically. ... Within this context it is vital to produce an updated politics of architecture in which the discipline is not merely reduced to a representation of ideal political concepts but conceived as an effective tool to produce change' (2008: 194). The angle was to 'mobilize the political in the vertical envelope as an expression of technical efficiencies', the same approach used for the ECB project (Zaera-Polo 2009: 127; Friedrich 2015). Architecture's engagement with politics was being moved toward the technical sphere of the envelope, which in turn was endowed with the ability to produce iconographic performance, expression, and even affect.

However, what was presented as a new form of political materialism also tended to align with the architectural outlook of most large organizations globally, as the go-to model for the generic, corporate high-rise at the turn of the millennium. In Frankfurt, the silhouette of the financial district, a couple of kilometers westward along the Main River, constitutes an inescapable term of comparison for the ECB headquarters. Kees Christiaanse, one of the renowned architects leading the jury of the ECB competition, told me that 'there was no wish to look like anything in the financial district' (2021). From his perspective, 'firstly, the buildings there are, apart from Commerzbank, not attractive; secondly, the ECB is a public institution, not a commercial institution; and thirdly, the ECB is supposed to guard everyone's financial safety'. The result of the competition, however, was a building that, to quote architectural historian Hauke Horn, aligned with the 'international iconography of financial high-rises' and did not show much of its 'political purpose' (2021).

The Commerzbank tower, which opened one year before the establishment of the ECB, was a particularly prominent point of reference (Krause 2016). From the full-height central atrium to the proposed 'hanging gardens', many of Coop Himmelb(l)au's choices seemed to reference Norman Foster's design for Commerzbank. Another important reference was the Deutsche Bank headquarters, which went through a transformative renovation process when the ECB was beginning construction. From a massing perspective, it was a similar example of a double-tower scheme, connected by a central atrium.

But the primary thread linking all these turn-of-the-millennium projects was the emphasis on the performance of the envelope. In 2008, the ECB stated that its new premises should be 30 % more energy-efficient than stipulated by the *Energieeinsparverordnung* (German energy saving directive). In 2009, Commerzbank received the Green Building Award. In 2011, Deutsche Bank was the first high-rise refurbishment project to receive the highest possible certifications—LEED Platinum and DGNB Gold—for their resource and energy efficiency. For Reinhard Frost, a historian working at the Deutsche

Bank archives, this endeavor was 'the hallmark of a new era and a highly visible expression of the financial and ecological identity of a global institution which has always been aware of its social responsibility' (2016: 50). In the middle of the debt crisis, as the misconduct of institutions like Deutsche Bank was being exposed to the world, financial and ecological concerns were swiftly juxtaposed, in the hope that a super-efficient envelope might help in the process of identity-(re)building (Caesar 2016).

Brutal Understatements

Although the material architecture of the ECB drew close to that of commercial banks, its institutional architecture had a different model, which was also based in Frankfurt: The Deutsche Bundesbank. Around the time of the Maastricht Treaty, when the project of monetary integration was laid out, the new European institution was explicitly modeled after Germany's central bank. As noted by Philipp Maier, the Bundesbank 'acted as the blueprint for the ECB' (2002: ii).

In addition to the fact that Germany had by far the strongest economy in the union, the Bundesbank represented a fitting model because of the way it had been structured after World War II. Following the collapse of the Nazi regime and its Reichsbank, the Americans redesigned central banking in Germany, creating a system akin to the Federal Reserve System of the United States. The first phase consisted of decentralization, through the establishment of regional central banks, coordinated by the Bank Deutscher Länder (Bank of the German States). Only in 1957, when the situation had stabilized, was this network replaced by a more centralized structure, with the establishment of the Bundesbank. Considering what had happened in the first half of the century, the new institution was the first central bank to be given full independence from government—one of the key principles that was later adopted by the ECB.

A new, independent central bank required a new headquarters, which was eventually built between 1967 and 1972 in Frankfurt's Nordend (Durth and Thies 2020). The ensemble, designed by Otto Apel, Hannsgeorg Beckert and Gilbert Becker, was centered on a 200-meter-long, horizontal, concrete slab, which was described by one of the bank's board members as a 'brutalist building' that 'radiates a strong sense of objectivity and functionality' (Deutsche Bundesbank 2016). At a symposium called 'Unloved Modernism', Wolfgang Voigt, former deputy director of the Deutsches Architekturmuseum, argued that, after the experience of the Reichsbank, 'any notion of the architecture being used as a statement of power was avoided at all costs' (2015).

As two institutions that claimed independence from government and originated from a difficult process of unification of state (or 'Land') banks, the Bundesbank and the ECB needed to avoid any overt statement of power. Naturally, the architectural outcome looked different. While the Bundesbank slab spoke the brutalist language of its time, the ECB tower was able to blend in with the corporate skyline of 21st-century Manhattan, as the city has been nicknamed (Sturm and Schmal 2014).

The analogy between the ECB design and the architecture of commercial banks and corporations fits into the narrative of those who see European integration solely as an economic project, a neoliberal endeavor driven by transnational capitalism—a reflection of what Zygmunt Bauman has described as the contemporary rift between power and politics. The situation, of course, is more complicated than that. European integration is a complex, non-linear process, where most of the progress happens through gradual spillovers, behind the scenes. Unlike most state institutions, the European institutions are careful not to project their power, because they fear that, given the complex and fragile nature of a supranational democracy, this power may be perceived as illegitimate. In the exercise of power, the goal is not to stand out but to blend in. Again, this is a feature that, for different reasons, European institutions share with post-WWII German institutions.

A good example pertaining to the ECB is the remarkable case of the design of the euro banknotes. Right before the launch of the competition for its headquarters, the ECB went through a painstaking process to define the iconography of the euro—a set of architectural images designed to appear as 'neutral' as possible, to be accepted by all member states (Fabbrini 2021b). This case clearly speaks to the hesitancy to present any clear architectural statement that may be perceived as overbearing or politically incorrect and that may generate a nationalist backlash.

According to Kees Christiaanse, the jury that selected Coop Himmelb(l)au's proposal saw the ECB as a 'service institution' and, therefore, was not looking for 'great monumentality' or 'extreme formal expression' (2021). For example, the jury commended the design concept by Johann Eisele, who was awarded the third prize in the competition, noting that 'it refrained from creating a unique and distinctive landmark for the ECB' but was 'efficient, technically and economically feasible and commendable' (ECB 2004: 20).

Francis Gross, one of the ECB executives who oversaw this endeavor from the inside and served as the secretary of the jury, was quite open in recognizing the will to understate the political and symbolic dimension of the architectural project. From his perspective, the emphasis on the functional and technical aspects of the building, rather than on its unique status as a supranational institution, spoke to the 'culture' of the ECB. On this issue, Gross made an interesting comment: 'we can actually see that an institution's approach to architecture reflects its approach to its mission, which can raise some concern' (2021).

Image and Identity

The functionalist culture of the ECB is well documented, and it is not surprising to see that it informed the institution's approach to architecture as well. A recent publication produced by the bank itself points to the fact that 'the competition brief, the final decision of the jury and the subsequent planning phases focused on the functionality and

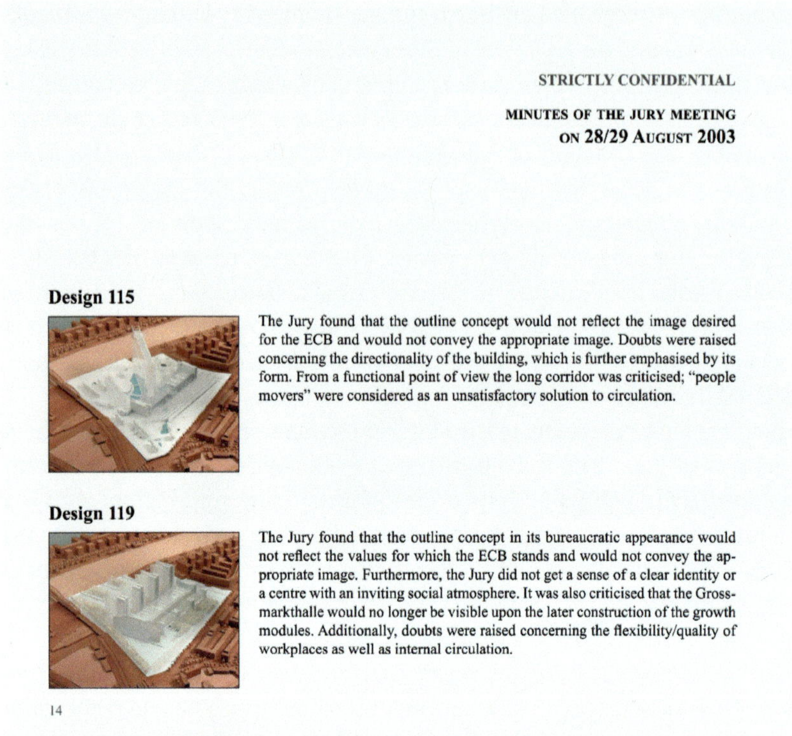

STRICTLY CONFIDENTIAL

MINUTES OF THE JURY MEETING
ON 28/29 AUGUST 2003

Design 115

The Jury found that the outline concept would not reflect the image desired for the ECB and would not convey the appropriate image. Doubts were raised concerning the directionality of the building, which is further emphasised by its form. From a functional point of view the long corridor was criticised; "people movers" were considered as an unsatisfactory solution to circulation.

Design 119

The Jury found that the outline concept in its bureaucratic appearance would not reflect the values for which the ECB stands and would not convey the appropriate image. Furthermore, the Jury did not get a sense of a clear identity or a centre with an inviting social atmosphere. It was also criticised that the Grossmarkthalle would no longer be visible upon the later construction of the growth modules. Additionally, doubts were raised concerning the flexibility/quality of workplaces as well as internal circulation.

14

3 Extract of the jury's evaluation of two design proposals, underlining the concern with the image of the ECB, 28–29 August 2003.
Source: European Central Bank.

sustainability of the new premises' (ECB 2020: 6). However, throughout this process, another important question kept arising: the question of the bank's image.

Of the 71 competition proposals, 24 were rejected for this reason (Fig. 3): 'The jury found that the outline concept would not reflect the values for which the ECB stands and would not convey the appropriate image' (ECB 2003b). On the contrary, the winning proposal by Coop Himmelb(l)au was praised by the jury for its ability to 'convey a powerful image and reflect the values of the ECB'. The ECB provided a list of values, which included transparency, communication, efficiency, and stability. As for the question of its image, however, there was never any explanation: no one articulated why any image was deemed appropriate or inappropriate.

In the case of the euro banknotes, this problem was addressed by carefully elaborating a set of architectural images that, while being realistic and somehow recognizable as European, did not represent any existing building. Interestingly, 10 years after the introduction of the euro, as construction of the ECB headquarters was beginning, the Dutch artist Robin Stam carried out an experimental project in the town of Spijkenisse, near Rotterdam, where he was able to build the 'fictional' bridges depicted on the banknotes (Stam 2011). This iconographic transfer from the two-dimensional realm of the banknote to the three-dimensional realm of the building also manifested itself on multiple occasions in the case of the ECB. Historically, this dynamic was the opposite: banknotes tended to depict images of important public buildings, representing the authority in charge of that currency. In the case of the euro, however, the banknote came before the building.

In 2008, as construction of the new ECB premises was about to begin, the Grossmarkthalle became the site of a large-scale light show during Luminale, a biennial festival for light art hosted by the City of Frankfurt. The installation, funded by the ECB and curated by Casa Magica, set out to highlight the transformation of the site by beaming a series of 'motifs' onto the building's façade (Casa Magica 2008). In Casa Magica's work, this type of installation is called 'architectural projection'. To highlight the market hall's future role as the ECB headquarters, its long façade was temporarily transformed by colorful projections, using motifs borrowed from banknotes.

Even before construction began, as the need to project some form of image presented itself, the solution was to take inspiration from banknotes. This idea is also evident in some of the renderings produced by Coop Himmelb(l)au. For example, a 2009 rendering of the press briefing room — one of the most prominent spaces in the new ECB premises, as well as the stage where the bank interacts with the public — features a large representation of a 5-euro banknote, which is hung behind the podium like a painting.

From rendering to reality, a similar move was implemented in another key space of the new building — the council room, the inner sanctum of the ECB's decision-making mechanism. As noted by one of Coop Himmelb(l)au's architects, there was little room for experimentation in terms of layout: the task was to replicate and optimize the council room of the previous ECB offices in the Eurotower — a conventional council room, with a central round table, that could be easily mistaken for the board room of any other bank (Schwed 2021). In fact, what is now known as the Eurotower was originally the seat of the Bank für Gemeinwirtschaft, built in the 1970s. The ECB council room was so non-specific that, shortly after its inauguration, the management of the bank considered turning it into a restaurant (Zaera-Polo 2009: 127).

The only concession to the specificity of the institution was the ceiling. As noted in an ECB brochure, 'the ceiling of the council room is unique: the architects call it the Europe ceiling — the aluminum elements depict a map of Europe (as shown on the euro banknotes) in an abstract way' (ECB 2014: 3). Displaying a map in the council room of a central bank is a common practice. A clear example is the council room of the Federal Reserve Board, which features a large map of the United States. Interestingly, a rare diverging case is the aforementioned Deutsche Bundesbank. In the central bank of a country that had just been defeated and divided, it would have been difficult to identify an appropriate map; instead, the council room was decorated with

4 ECB council room, featuring the so-called "Europe ceiling" at the end of construction, 21 October 2014.
Source: European Central Bank / Jens Meyer.

surrealist tapestries by Max Ernst — an unintentionally fitting representation of the chaotic state of post-war Germany (Herget 2016: 54).

The ECB decided to take on the challenge of map-displaying because it was perceived as the least problematic, lowest-common-denominator image. But to make it work, the map had to be broken down and deformed, its details radically blurred, especially its borders, to the point where it became almost illegible (Fig. 4). The euro banknotes and coins had already performed this operation ten years earlier and, again, served as the basis for the creation of images in the new building.

At a speech during the launch of the euro in 1999, Wim Duisenberg, the first president of the ECB, made the case that 'a currency is far more than just a medium of exchange; a currency is also part of the identity of people; it reflects what they have in common, now and in the future' (Iley and Lewis 2013: 220; see also Buscha, Mueller, and Page 2017). In the absence of a clear political project, the euro was bestowed with the monumental responsibility of generating a common identity, including the difficult effort of elaborating images that could fill the EU's iconographic vacuum and fuel future building projects. At the ceremony for the laying of the foundation stone of the ECB building, in the spring of 2010, the president of the bank, along with the architect and the mayor of Frankfurt, solemnly placed a set of euro banknotes into a metal box that would be laid into the stone (Fig. 5). While it was not unusual to put money in foundation stones, this case was particularly significant. The 'house of the euro', as it was often called, was conceptually and physically built upon a banknote (Draghi 2015).

5 President Trichet places a set of euro banknotes into the foundation stone of the EBC building, 19 May 2010.
Source: European Central Bank / Robert Metsch.

Rituals and Riots

Even though the ECB project, much like the EU itself, was framed in functional, economic terms, certain political dynamics continued to infiltrate the site, sometimes in unexpected ways, especially as the institution adopted an increasingly central political role during the financial crisis. While the ECB tried to focus the competition on technical, utilitarian issues, several public ceremonies throughout the building process forced all actors to address a different set of issues, venturing into the uncomfortable realm of the symbolic and, in one way or another, the political.

The first such ceremonies occurred in the spring of 2008, in the Schwanenhalle of the Römer, Frankfurt's 15th-century town hall. With the backdrop of a large Renaissance tapestry featuring a battle scene, the mayor of Frankfurt handed over the building permit to the ECB president in front of the media, displaying the transfer of power from the municipal to the supranational authority. The mayor was also involved in the laying of the foundation stone in 2010—an articulate ceremony that primarily displayed the merger of multiple national central banks into a single European institution. After the set of euro banknotes had been placed into the foundation stone, the directors of all the national central banks of the EU walked by the stone, one by one, and laid down a copy of a newspaper from their country. Wolf Prix, CEO of Coop Himmelb(l)au, was also involved, as he was asked to add the plans of the building into the foundation stone. Resting together within the stone, these architectural drawings constituted the joining of supranational tokens (the banknotes) with national tokens (the newspapers).

Two years later, in 2012, an even more theatrical ceremony marked the topping out of the building's structure. In line with a tradition that spans most of northern

6 Topping-out ceremony at the ECB building, 20 September 2012.
Source: European Central Bank / Klaus Helbig.

Europe, the builders raised a topping-out wreath and placed it atop the tower (Fig. 6). Again, one by one, the governors of the national central bank hung the flag of their country on the wreath, which had already been adorned with blue ribbons displaying the EU flag. While the foundation stone was meant to be buried forever, this was a temporary, highly visible display. Made of pine branches and clad in flags, the wreath was shaped like a building—a small pavilion that embodied the process of supranationalization behind the ECB. Even if only for a few hours, a purely symbolic, temporary pavilion designed to express the uniqueness of this institution, as well as the political dynamics behind it, was placed on top of the actual structure.

When the project was completed, in March 2015, another ceremony was performed inside the new building, with all the local and European authorities coming together to celebrate. Meanwhile, outside the building, a different set of political forces had begun to mobilize, and, as the ribbon was being cut, a major riot exploded in the neighborhood. Activists from all over Europe had assembled in front of this new architectural landmark to protest the austerity measures carried out by the ECB during and after the financial crisis. They did not see the ECB as a neutral service institution, making technical decisions: they saw it as a political actor. Although the goal of the institution was to understate its political dimension, the new building was immediately turned into a site of political engagement by EU citizens.

Since its inauguration day, the gardens surrounding the ECB high-rise have been occupied by countless rallies and demonstrations. One of the most recent was a Greenpeace demonstration, in which two activists paraglided onto the roof of the building and unfolded a large banner, covering the super-green façade with the following message: 'Stop funding climate killers' (Fig. 7).

While analyzing the institutional messaging at these events and ceremonies during the construction process, one may notice that the ECB itself gradually started to reas-

7 Greenpeace paragliders hang a banner on the façade of the ECB building, 10 March 2021.
Source: Greenpeace / Felix Schmitt.

sess its own role and priorities. When the ECB acquired the site of the Grossmarkthalle, the reason given to the public was that it was 'the most economically viable' (ECB 2020: 4). At the building permit ceremony in the Rathaus, ECB president Trichet argued that the most important task was the preservation of the historic market hall, minimizing the impact of the new tower (Trichet 2008). Two years later, at the foundation stone ceremony, he said that the priority was to provide the bank with 'a functional headquarters, while keeping the building costs within the foreseen budget and using our resources responsibly' (Trichet 2010). At the topping-out ceremony, the main speech was given by Jörg Asmussen, member of the ECB executive board, who focused heavily on budgetary issues, detailing all the costs of construction. In the end, the building was 350 million euros over budget (Pagliacolo 2015).

But what is worth noting is that, by the time the inauguration came around, the institutional language had started to change. The mayor of Frankfurt began by stating that 'this project was not just about the balance sheet, but about the European idea as a whole' (Feldman 2015). He also pointed to Frankfurt's history as an arena for open political debate and criticism of 'the excesses of financial capitalism', drawing a connection between the Frankfurt School and the ECB. The deputy prime minister of Hesse, the Bundesland in which Frankfurt is located, then took the stage and discussed, among other things, the austerity measures of the ECB and the economic situation in Greece. The ceremony culminated with the remarks of the then ECB president, Mario Draghi. While protesters were gathering outside, he talked about the changing role of the ECB, arguing for the 'need to reconcile the economics of integration with the politics of integration' (Draghi 2015). He noted that 'the more decision-making over economic issues moves to the European level, the more democracy needs to move with it'. Part of this process of democratization involved the grounding of the institution in a specific location — a building around which citizens can gather and make their voices heard.

Architecture and Myopia

In her 2017 book *Five Ways to Make Architecture Political*, Albena Yaneva argued that buildings should no longer be seen as 'political symbols or embodiments of big political forces' (2017: 7). Similarly to Zaera-Polo, she separated architecture from traditional, overshadowing theories of power — related to ideology, state, nation, government, or activism — and made the case that the political can be generated and explored at the 'myopic, microscopic level of the practice'. The inner workings of architecture in practice were therefore attributed a great deal of political agency.

The ECB competition is one of those cases that call for a significant scaling down of most assumptions regarding both what architects are allowed to do and what architects can do. The development of the Holocaust memorial is a good example of the degree to which the ECB endeavored to keep architects away from the political. To commemorate the darkest chapter in the history of the Grossmarkthalle, when its basement was used as a gathering place for the deportation of Jewish families, the ECB decided to include a memorial in its new premises. The design of the most symbolic space in the new headquarters, however, was divorced from the architectural competition. A separate competition was organized for the memorial in collaboration with the City of Frankfurt and the local Jewish community (ECB 2009). The design and construction process of the building and the memorial ran in parallel, and both were completed in 2015, but the projects had little interaction with each other.

At the inauguration of the memorial, the space was presented as 'a symbol of why we can never again risk to split apart' (Draghi 2015). The entire process of economic and political integration had been set up in the aftermath of World War II as a direct response to the horrors of nationalism pushed to its extremes. What happened in those basements across Germany and other countries is the reason the EU was created. While the basement of this new supranational institution in Frankfurt was literally one of the sites where those horrors unfolded, the architectural competition stayed clear of that space, which was addressed as a separate design task. This was the clearest possible opportunity to reflect on the history of European integration and remind everybody how and why institutions like the ECB had been established. None of the 2002 competition proposals could seize this opportunity, as this loaded topic had been taken off the architects' table.

This case also highlights limitations that do not depend on external forces. The outcome of the ECB competition was determined not only by the institution's unwillingness to expose itself and make a political statement through architecture, but also by the difficulty, on the part of many architects, to fully grasp the political stakes of this endeavor. Of the 71 architectural firms that took part in the competition, how many

ECB-UNRESTRICTED

116
Grüntuch / Ernst Architekten
Berlin, Germany
Armand Grüntuch
Almut Ernst

Outline Concept
"The new ECB building symbolises the strength of joined power in many aspects. The building is not a solitaire, but an ensemble of elements that form a significant silhouette. As a building for a supra-national Institution it symbolises the emerging new challenges and dynamic energies of the future in the common European market.

8 Extract of one of the 71 proposals submitted to the first round of the ECB competition — the only proposal that used the term "supranational," 2003.
Source: European Central Bank.

knew how European integration worked or how a supranational institution differed from other institutions?

Only one of the short 'concept outlines' that each participant had to submit alluded to the uniqueness of EU power and used the term 'supranational' (ECB 2003a: 17) (Fig. 8). The second closest attempt was a proposal that described the ECB as a 'supra-regional' institution. Other proposals reveal a misunderstanding of the logic behind the institution. For example, Miralles and Tagliabue addressed the site of the ECB as 'the base/landscape for the different/individual pavilions/countries' (ECB 2003a: 64). Rather than a place where national powers could merge into a supranational entity, the ECB was treated as an international fair, where each country had its own pavilion, à la Biennale. But the most common move was to sprinkle some symbolism in the landscaping around the new building: the firms that proposed some form of garden, with trees or flowers representing all EU member states, include SOM, NHT, BRT, KHR, and United Architects / UN Studio.

Notably, a significant portion of the competition participants, the architects at the top of the international game, belonged to the '68 generation — a generation shaped by political activism. For example, Coop Himmelb(l)au was founded in May 1968 (Lavin 2010). Forty years later, when a unique opportunity to reflect on a new form of power appeared, many proposals revealed a lack of interest or competence to address these types of political questions and produce meaningful statements about them, potentially embracing a critical role.

Representation and Depoliticization

Theatrics and symbols have historically played a key role in the architecture of financial institutions and especially central banks (Bergdoll 2001; Belfoure 2005). In a field characterized by immaterial transactions and high-risk exchanges, the body of the institution was often used as a stage to represent stability and instill a sense of confidence in the users. In the process, architecture was called on to manufacture a tangible image that could help identify this form of power, which most people did not fully understand. Dating back to the 18th century, the Bank of England led the way in this arena, showing that the architecture of money was primarily a problem of representation (Abramson 2005). The project developed by John Soane was essentially a mise-en-scène—a sequence of aesthetic experiences, based on references from the history of architecture, which produced a space that conveyed a certain aura and, therefore, could elevate obscure bureaucratic acts to the level of public ritual.

This type of engagement between architecture and power, however, presupposes a degree of clarity and complicity between the public officials and the designers about the identity of the institution and its political mission. When that is the case, the political effects of the building can be controlled and directed in specific ways. Again, in the case of the Bank of England, the architectural project was clearly part of a larger political project, centered on the notion of empire and its commercial underpinnings. In *The Wealth of Nations*, which came out during that time, Adam Smith made the case that this institution was not 'an ordinary bank' but rather 'a great engine of state' (1776: 249). Soane shared this vision and saw architecture as a key mechanism of this engine. From this perspective, the bank became one of the prime testing grounds for the definition of a modern British architecture, aiming to delineate a concrete representation of national character.

While it belongs to a different era, this example is significant because it shows not only the political dimension of this type of institutional architecture but also its historical entrenchment in the dynamics of nation-building. Notably, both forces are antithetical to European integration, which was framed as a project of depoliticization and supranationalization. After World War II, the political was very much understood in a Schmittian sense, as a fundamentally agonistic, conflictual dynamic that led to what everyone had just experienced in a very real way: war between nations (Schmitt 1976; Fusco and Zivanaris 2021).

The withdrawal from the sphere of the political and the push to reframe national identity are key to understanding the difficulty, on the part of the European institutions, of producing a public architecture that can perform a representational function. Given the complex balance in which the ECB exists, architecture is perceived as a minefield, precisely because of its symbolic potential. The struggle to define a handful of images of (fictional) buildings for the euro banknotes had been a preview, on a small scale, of this predicament. Buildings can easily come across as political statements or, at a minimum, are vulnerable to being turned into sites of engagement and confrontation, even when their makers and users have no such intention (Mouffe et al. 2014).

From this perspective, the case of the ECB highlights two diverging dynamics. On the one hand, the outlook of the institution aligned with an emerging position in the architectural discourse, which was moving away from traditional modes of representation and closer to an object-oriented philosophy (Gage 2015). From this point of view, one could argue that the super-efficient, hyperbolic envelope designed by Coop Himmelb(l)au is actually the perfect representation of an institution that wants to be measured by its technical performance and that struggles to define and express its deeper identity.

On the other hand, the limitations of such alignment came to the fore as soon as the design process began. While approaching this type of building as a reflection of political forces had become somewhat taboo for both the architects and the bank's officials, issues of meaning and image reentered through the back door. Given the importance of the ECB in the framework of European governance, multiple forces tried to fill the semantic space that was left blank by those who drove the project. The example of the Greenpeace demonstration, among others, shows that the absence of endogenous messaging leads to representations from the outside, as the envelope unintentionally becomes a screen for exogenous projections. The technocratic vision of an institutional architecture that frames its power in terms of efficiency and performance clashes with the democratic demand for legible symbols and rituals. Outlining what the institution (and its building) does can only provide a partial answer to the inevitable question of what the institution (and the building) stands for.

References

Abramson, D. 2005. *Building the Bank of England: Money, Architecture, Society, 1694–1942*. New Haven: Yale University Press.

Alesina, A. and Giavazzi, F. 2020. *Europe and the Euro*. Chicago: University of Chicago Press.

Arendt, H. 1958. *The Human Condition*. Chicago: University of Chicago Press.

Athanassiou, P. 2018. The Institutional Architecture and Tasks of the European Central Bank since the Crisis: An Overview. *Centro Studi sul Federalismo — Research Papers*.

Belfoure, C. 2005. *Monuments to Money: The Architecture of American Banks*. Jefferson: McFarland & Company.

Bergdoll, B. 2001. *European Architecture, 1750–1890*. Oxford: Oxford University Press.

Buscha, F, Mueller, D, and Page L. 2017. Can a Common Currency Foster a Shared Social Identity Across Different Nations? The Case of the Euro. *European Economic Review*, 100: 318–336. https://doi.org/10.1016/j.euroecorev.2017.08.011

Caesar, E. 2016. Deutsche Bank's $10-Billion Scandal. *The New Yorker*, 29 August. Available at https://www.newyorker.com/magazine/2016/08/29/deutsche-banks-10-billion-scandal [Last accessed 31 January 2023].

Casa Magica. 2008. Architectural Projection at Luminale. *Casa Magica* website. Available at https://casamagica.de/Examples/Luminale2008/engl/index.html [Last accessed 31 January 2023].

Chipperfield, D, Souto de Moura, E, Herzog, J and de Meuron, P. 1994. *The Bank: Three Architectural Concepts for the Future*. Ivrea: Olivetti.

Christiaanse, K. 2021. Interview by Sebastiano Fabbrini, October.

Coop Himmelb(l)au. n. d. European Central Bank — Project Information. Available at https://coop-himmelblau.at/projects/european-central-bank-ecb/ [Last accessed 31 January 2023].

Deutsche Bundesbank. 2016. Bundesbank Central Office: A Symbol of the Bank's Stability Culture. Available at https://www.bundesbank.de/en/tasks/topics/bundesbank-central-office-a-symbol-of-the-bank-s-stability-culture-667020 [Last accessed 31 January 2023].

Dinan, D. (ed.) 2006. *Origins and Evolution of the European Union*. Oxford: Oxford University Press.

Draghi, M. 2015. *Speech at the Inauguration of the New ECB Premises*, 18 March. ECB Archives.

Durth, W and Thies, N. 2020. *The Past Becomes the Future: The Deutsche Bundesbank's Central Office in Frankfurt am Main*. Frankfurt: Deutsche Bundesbank.

ECB [European Central Bank]. 1998. *Headquarters Agreement between the Government of the Federal Republic of Germany and the European Central Bank Concerning the Seat of the European Central Bank*, 18 September. ECB Archives.

ECB [European Central Bank]. 2002. *Competition Brief — Urban Planning and Architectural Design Competition for the New ECB Premises in Frankfurt am Main, Germany*. ECB Archives.

ECB [European Central Bank]. 2003a. *New ECB Premises — Architectural Design Competition — Design Proposals — First Phase*. ECB Archives.

ECB [European Central Bank]. 2003b. *New ECB Premises — Urban Planning and Architectural Design Competition — First Phase of the Competition — Minutes of the Jury Meeting*, 28–29 August. ECB Archives.

ECB [European Central Bank]. 2004. *New ECB Premises — Urban Planning and Architectural Design Competition — Second Phase of the Competition — Minutes of the Jury Meeting*, 12–13 February. ECB Archives.

ECB [European Central Bank]. 2009. *Competition Brief — Memorial at the Frankfurt Grossmarkthalle*. ECB Archives.

ECB [European Central Bank]. 2014. *New ECB Premises: Facts and Figures*. ECB Archives.

ECB [European Central Bank]. 2020. *Main Building: from Conception to Completion*. Frankfurt: European Central Bank.

Fabbrini, S. 2021a. Whatever Happened to Supranational Architecture? *Ardeth*, 7: 85–105. https://doi.org/10.17454/ardeth07.06

Fabbrini, S. 2021b. Architecting the Euro. *Architectural Histories*, 9. https://doi.org/10.5334/ah.473

Frankfurter Allgemeine Zeitung. 2015. *EZB Eröffnet Restaurant in Ihrem Neubau*. April 1. https://www.faz.net/aktuell/rhein-main/frankfurt/gastronomie-ezb-eroeffnet-restaurant-in-ihrem-neubau-13516884.html#void

Feldman, P. 2015. *Speech at the Inauguration of the New ECB Premises*, 18 March. ECB Archives.

Friedrich, J. 2015. Europa am Main. *Bauwelt*, 4: 14–25.

Frost, R. 2016. Taunusanlage 12, Frankfurt am Main: More Than Just Steel and Concrete. *The European Association for Banking and Financial History Bulletin: Architecture and Finance*: 50–51.

Fusco, G, and Zivanaris, M. 2021. The Neutralisation of the Political: Carl Schmitt and the Depoliticisation of Europe. *Journal of Contemporary European Studies*, 30(2): 363–378. https://doi.org/10.1080/14782804.2021.1873109

Gage, MF. 2015. Killing Simplicity: Object-Oriented Philosophy in Architecture. *Log*, 33: 95–106.

Gross, F. 2021. Interview by Sebastiano Fabbrini, October.

Hein, C. 2004. *The Capital of Europe: Architecture and Urban Planning for the European Union*. Westport: Praeger.

Heisenberg, D. and Richmond, A. 2002. Supranational Institution-Building in the European Union. *Journal of European Public Policy*, 9(2): 201–218. https://doi.org/10.1080/13501760110120228

Herget, R. 2016. The Deutsche Bundesbank: Its Architecture and Art. *The European Association for Banking and Financial History Bulletin: Architecture and Finance*: 52–54.

Herzog & de Meuron, 1994. Projects: 103 Contribution to Die Bank, Three Architectural Concepts for the Future, Deutsches Architekturmuseum, Frankfurt am Main, Germany. https://www.herzogdemeuron.com/projects/103-contribution-to-die-bank-three-architectural-concepts-for-the-future/.

Horn, H. 2021. Interview by Sebastiano Fabbrini, September.

Howarth, D. and Loedel, P. 2005. *The European Central Bank: The New European Leviathan?* New York: Palgrave.

Iley, R and Lewis, M. 2013. *Global Finance after the Crisis*. Northampton: Elgar.

Krause, D. 2016. Commerzbank and Frankfurt am Main. *The European Association for Banking and Financial History Bulletin: Architecture and Finance*: 47–49.

Lamant, L. 2018. *Bruxelles Chantiers: Une Critique Architecturale de l'Europe*. Montreal. Lux.

Lavin, S. 2010. Revolution 9. *Coop Himmelb(l)au: HS#9*. Munich: Prestel.

Maier, P. 2002. *Political Pressure, Rhetoric and Monetary Policy: Lessons for the European Central Bank*. Northampton: Elgar.

Mouffe, C., Martin, R., Aureli, P. V., Whiting, S., and Weizman, I. 2014. *How Is Architecture Political?* Symposium at the Architectural Association. Available at https://www.youtube.com/watch?v=nZxThrCyKI0 [Last accessed 31 January 2023].

Pagliacolo, E. 2015. The European Central Bank by Coop Himmelb(l)au. *Azure*, 29 January. Available at https://www.azuremagazine.com/article/european-central-bank-coop-himmelblau/ [Last accessed 31 January 2023].

Schmitt, C. 1976. *The Concept of the Political*. New Brunswick: Rutgers University Press.

Schwed, T. 2021, Interview by Sebastiano Fabbrini, October

Smith, A. 1776. *The Wealth of Nations*. London: Strahan and Cadell.

Stam, R. 2011. The Bridges of Europe. Available at https://thebridgesofeurope.tumblr.com/ [Last accessed 31 January 2023].

Sterken, S. 2015. Bruxelles, Ville de Bureaux: Le Berlaymont et la Transformation du Quartier Léopold. *Journées du Patrimoine, Région de Bruxelles-Capitale*, 15–16 : 102–117.

Sturm, P and Schmal, P. (eds.) 2014. *High-Rise City Frankfurt: Buildings and Visions since 1945*. Munich: Prestel.

Trichet, J. 2008. *The Handing Over of the Building Permit for the New European Central Bank Premises by the City of Frankfurt — Introductory Statement*, 6 May. ECB Archives.

Trichet, J. 2010. *New ECB Premises: Ceremony of the Laying of the Foundation Stone — Welcome Address*, 19 May. ECB Archives.

Voigt, W. 2015. *Unloved Modernism.* Symposium hosted by the Deutsche Bundesbank.

Wiggins, RZ, Wedow, M and Metrick, A. 2019. European Banking Union: The Single Supervisory Mechanism. *The Journal of Financial Crises*, 1(3): 113–129. https://elischolar.library.yale.edu/journal-of-financial-crises/vol1/iss3/7

Yaneva, A. 2017. *Five Ways to Make Architecture Political: An Introduction to the Politics of Design Practice*. London: Bloomsbury.

Zaera-Polo, A. 2008. The Politics of The Envelope. *Log*, 13–14: 193–207.

Zaera-Polo, A. 2009. The Politics of The Envelope, Part II. *Log*, 16: 97–132.

Chapter 5
Architecting the Euro

Abstract

This chapter explores an obscure project in architectural history that a bank commissioned an interdisciplinary group of intellectuals to undertake in the mid-1990s. The task was to provide models to the participants in a design competition for the banknotes of a new currency—models that were not to be reproduced but only stylized, concealing any specific historical reference. After the winner was determined through an opinion poll, an unexpected by-product was the construction of actual buildings modeled after the stylized architectures on the banknotes. The distinctiveness of this process, and the reason for its complexity, lies in the fact that, contrary to what one may expect when discussing architecture and money (especially architecture on money), everything had to operate on a supranational level. The currency in question was the euro, which replaced the national currencies and on 1 January 2002 became the common currency of twelve European states: Austria, Belgium, Finland, France, Germany, Greece, Ireland, Italy, Luxembourg, the Netherlands, Portugal and Spain. The organization behind this endeavor was the European Monetary Institute, in collaboration with Gallup Europe. Its task force was asked to produce a historical survey of European architecture, whatever that might mean. In all the documents associated with this project, the key principle repeated is: 'It is imperative that national bias is avoided' (EMI 1996: 2). As architecture and, more specifically, architectural history had been working in the opposite direction for centuries, this is a unique opportunity to explore how our discipline negotiated the process of *nation-unbuilding* and the emergence of a new, supranational structure of power in Europe.

> *'When bankers get together for dinner, they discuss Art.*
> *When artists get together for dinner, they discuss Money'.*
> Oscar Wilde

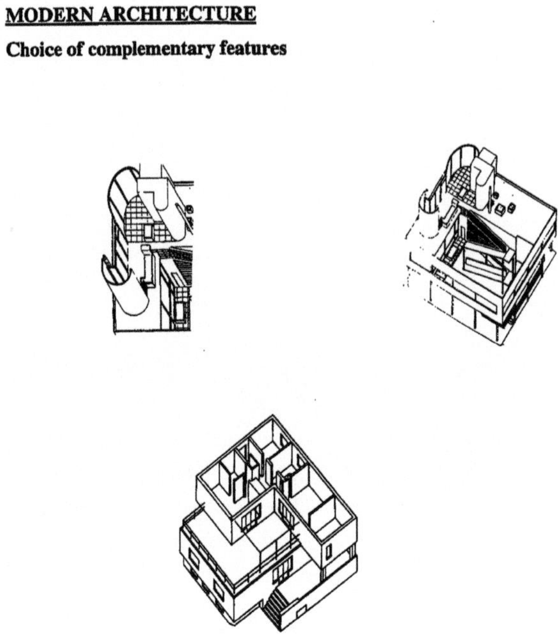

1 Feature Selection Advisory Group, *Selection of Design Features for the European Banknote Series*, 1995. Detail of three "complementary features" for the Euro banknotes.
Source: Archives of the European Central Bank.

Theming the Euro: Issues of Style, Matters of State

The first step toward designing a common European currency was a matter of 'theming'. The challenge was to identify an overarching theme that spoke to the idea of a united Europe. While the initial instinct was to lean on Europe's vast historical heritage, the past was a minefield, a history of conflict, mostly colored by the dynamics of the state. How could an entity that had been built to put an end to that history also manipulate it and extract an image of unity?

The euro project began in earnest after the signing of the Maastricht Treaty in 1992, the agreement responsible for the creation of the European Union (Mulhearn and Vane 2008; Chang 2009; Heinonen 2015). In the same year, the governors of the central banks of the states involved in this process established the Working Group on Printing and Issuing a European Banknote. Pursuing the goal of monetary unification also required a new supranational institution. The intergovernmental committee of bank governors that had supervised financial matters since the 1960s had to be replaced by an organization that could properly oversee the transition toward a common currency. The European Monetary Institute began operations in 1994, paving the way for the establishment of the European Central Bank, which took over its functions in 1998.

Upon meeting in November 1994 in Basel to discuss how the design of the new banknotes was to be organized, the Working Group on Printing and Issuing a European Banknote decided to assemble a team of 'experts from appropriate disciplines, including historians, art experts, psychologists and both banknote and general design professionals' that could come up with a series of possible themes for the euro notes (TSAG 1995: 3). This team took the name of Theme Selection Advisory Group.

The group comprised fifteen members. As they had to be nominated by the central banks, most of these members were the heads of the design section, the graphic designers or the keepers of the collections of said banks. There was only one art historian: Jaap Bolten, an expert on Dutch prints and drawings from the sixteenth and seventeenth centuries.

As evidenced by the confidential report sent to the European Monetary Institute in May 1995, the Theme Selection Advisory Group considered eighteen themes for the new banknote series and ranked them from best to worst (Fig. 2). The report included a detailed description and a 'critique' of each theme, illustrating its advantages and disadvantages. One of the main criteria was that of 'acceptability': the group used the hypothetical example of a banknote bearing a portrait of Napoleon to show how certain images would be accepted in some countries (one in particular) and rejected in others (TSAG 1995: 4).

The preferred theme was called Ages and Styles of Europe. The proposal was to have 'portraits of ordinary men and women' on one side of the banknotes and 'architectural styles' on the other. Both the people and the architecture were to be 'completely nameless', to avoid possible 'traps and pitfalls'. The goal was to 'convey, without specific reference to any given building, a clear message on the architectural richness and unity of Europe' (TSAG 1995: 7).

Ages and Styles of Europe was not the only theme that engaged with architecture. Among other proposals was a particularly significant theme called Monuments, ranked thirteenth in the report (Fig. 3). It suggested representations of iconic buildings, such as the Parthenon and the Eiffel Tower. The advisors compiled a long list of disadvantages, noting that only a handful of member states would be represented, that most monuments convey different symbolic messages in different countries and, most importantly, that very few monuments are linked with 'the idea of Europe' (TSAG 1995: 37).

It is quite difficult to find a monument in Europe that was not conceived according to or retroactively steeped in some kind of nationalist narrative (Hobsbawm and Ranger 1993; Choay 2001). The advisory group argued that the only way to avoid these problems was to illustrate 'styles of monuments' rather than specific buildings, which was essentially the idea of the first theme (TSAG 1995: 37). From the beginning of this process, stylization was identified as the operation that could unlock the iconographic labyrinth.

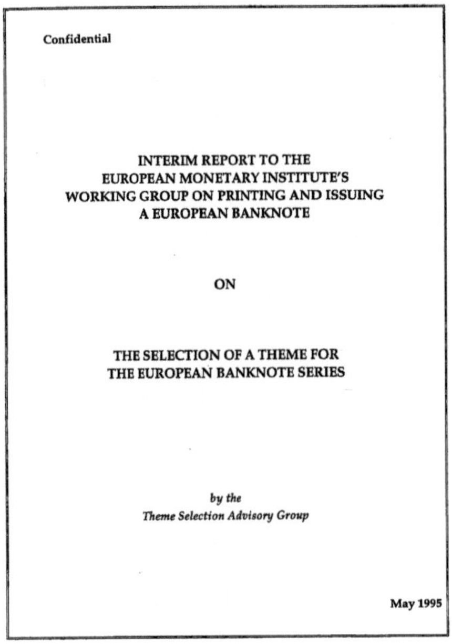

Confidential

INTERIM REPORT TO THE
EUROPEAN MONETARY INSTITUTE'S
WORKING GROUP ON PRINTING AND ISSUING
A EUROPEAN BANKNOTE

ON

THE SELECTION OF A THEME FOR
THE EUROPEAN BANKNOTE SERIES

by the
Theme Selection Advisory Group

May 1995

2 Theme Selection Advisory Group, *Selection of a Theme for the European Banknote Series*, 1995. Cover of the final, confidential report.
Source: Archives of the European Central Bank.

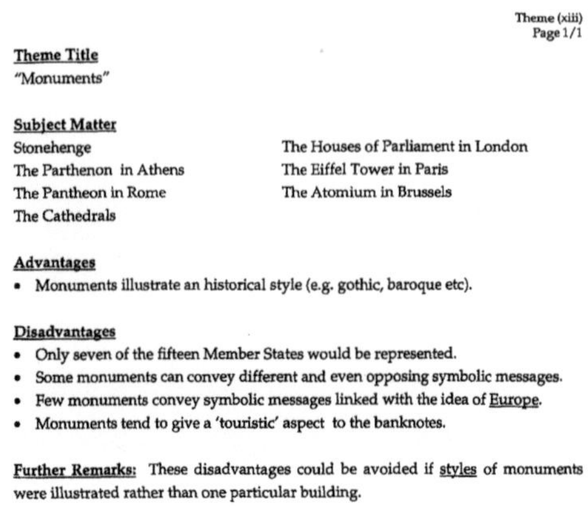

Theme (xiii)
Page 1/1

Theme Title
"Monuments"

Subject Matter
Stonehenge
The Parthenon in Athens
The Pantheon in Rome
The Cathedrals
The Houses of Parliament in London
The Eiffel Tower in Paris
The Atomium in Brussels

Advantages
- Monuments illustrate an historical style (e.g. gothic, baroque etc).

Disadvantages
- Only seven of the fifteen Member States would be represented.
- Some monuments can convey different and even opposing symbolic messages.
- Few monuments convey symbolic messages linked with the idea of Europe.
- Monuments tend to give a 'touristic' aspect to the banknotes.

Further Remarks: These disadvantages could be avoided if styles of monuments were illustrated rather than one particular building.

3 Theme Selection Advisory Group, *Selection of a Theme for the European Banknote Series*, 1995. Description of the thirteenth theme, tiled *Monuments*.
Source: Archives of the European Central Bank.

The logic of stylization, however, had itself been historically rooted in the dynamics of nation-building throughout most of Europe. While stylization sprang from the universalizing ethos of the Enlightenment and was initially put to work as a method for systematizing the past (as exemplified by Winckelmann's *Geschichte*), it took on additional meaning at the beginning of the nineteenth century, becoming a tool for the construction of national representations (Harloe 2013). As noted by Barry Bergdoll, this was the period in which 'issues of style became matters of state' (Bergdoll 2000: 141).[1] A definition provided by Heinrich Hübsch in the pamphlet *In What Style Should We Build?* is quite telling: 'Style means something general, applicable to all buildings of a nation' (Hübsch 1992: 66).

1 The recent controversy surrounding the proposal to enforce a single architectural style for all new federal buildings in the United States shows how issues of style still permeate the dispute between nationalism and its opponents.

Feature Selection: Political Correctness and Postmodernization

The second phase in the development of the euro revolved around an intricate debate on which 'features' could form the overarching idea of the selected theme. Countering a pattern that had long characterized the design of banknotes, the common currency turned away from anthropomorphic representation, which, unlike architecture, was ill-suited to the logic of stylization.

In June 1995, the Working Group on Printing and Issuing a European Banknote accepted the recommendations of the advisory group and decided to move forward with the theme Ages and Styles of Europe. But, at the same meeting, the working group determined that a design competition based on this theme required additional preparatory work. The result was the creation of a second team, called the Feature Selection Advisory Group, which this time needed to include 'members with specific experience in art and architectural history'. The group had three and a half months to produce 'a written report with appropriate illustrations' on the theme (FSAG 1995: 14).

Given the tight schedule and the fact that, again, the 'experts' needed to be nominated by the national central banks, twelve out of fifteen theme group members also took part in the Feature Selection Advisory Group. Italy and Finland opted for change and nominated two art historians: Nicole Dacos Crifò from the University of Siena and Aimo Reitala from the University of Turku. However, despite the nature of the theme, the group included no architectural historians and had only two members with a degree in architecture: José Pedro Martins Barata, the president of the Portuguese Design Center, and John Voncken, an architect who worked for the Service des Sites et Monuments Nationaux at Luxembourg's Ministry of Culture.

The first task was to perform the act of periodization implied by the theme Ages and Styles of Europe (Fig. 4). As the European Monetary Institute had already determined that the new currency would have seven denominations, the group had to divide the historical matter at hand into seven 'ages and styles' (Heinonen 2015: 39–53). The final report acknowledged that the group had initially identified ten periods but then found a way to cut it down to the required number: 'Classical, Romanesque, Gothic, Renaissance, Baroque and Rococo, iron and glass architecture, and modern architecture' (FSAG 1995: 3).

Although most members of the feature group had also been part of the theme group, the former ended up challenging some of the principles outlined by the latter. The main bone of contention was the notion that the features on the banknotes had to be 'anonymous'. Such skepticism found its way into the introduction to the report: 'Although opinions are divided among the experts, the majority view is that the European banknotes should depict parts of real buildings; the artists and graphic designers should not be allowed to produce a freely invented representation of an architectural style' (FSAG 1995: 2).

The group also raised another fundamental objection that the European Monetary Institute came to share. As previously noted, the concept of Ages and Styles

2. Identification of architectural styles

Following an initial examination of ten architectural styles the Group agreed that features of the architectural styles relating to the following seven periods should be represented on the notes:

Period	Style
8th century BC to 4th century AD	Classical (Greek and Roman)
11th century to 12th century	Romanesque
13th century to 14th century	Gothic
15th and 16th centuries	Renaissance
1600 to 1750	Baroque and rococo
1850 to 1914	Iron and glass architecture
from the 1930s onwards	Modern architecture

4 Feature Selection Advisory Group, *Selection of Design Features for the European Banknote Series*, 1995. Identification of the seven "periods" and "styles."
Source: Archives of the European Central Bank.

of Europe was to combine representations of architectural styles with portraits of ordinary people 'taken from European paintings, drawings, sketches, etc.' The advisors, however, pointed out that it was impossible to 'check the political correctness' of these figures (FSAG 1995: 9). Thereafter, the entire design process was steered away from portraits and centered on architecture alone. In fact, when the euro was put into circulation in 2002, one of its most innovative features was the absence of human representation.

In his research on currency iconography, Jacques Hymans assembled a database of more than a thousand European banknotes, from the early nineteenth century to the 1980s and showed how this iconographic space had been dominated by human figures, which had evolved over time from mythical symbols of states in flowing robes to portraits of famous individuals, such as painters and composers (Hymans 2004). One of the most common approaches adopted the 'masters and masterpieces scheme', which featured images of 'great men' on one side of the banknote and related 'great buildings' on the other (Hymans 2004: 21). This scheme is also found in the banknotes of other federal systems to which the European Union is often compared. For instance, the US dollar features images of presidents and prominent public buildings, such as the White House and the Lincoln Memorial. Another significant example is the Swiss Confederation, which in 1995 introduced a new banknote series centered on famous personalities in the arts and their work: the first note in the series (10 francs) featured a portrait of Le Corbusier on one side and drawings of his Chandigarh project on the other (Fig. 5).

In a speech titled 'The Euro: A Currency without a State', the first chief economist of the European Central Bank, Otmar Issing, defined the euro as 'a unique experi-

5 Le Corbusier's 10-Franc note, 1995. This banknote was discontinued in 2017, due to protests regarding Le Corbusier's affinities with fascism and the Vichy government. It was replaced by a note aiming to represent Switzerland's "organizational talent and punctuality."
Source: Swiss National Bank.

ence in history', considering that, on the one hand, it was based on a supranational monetary order and, on the other hand, political union was limited and sovereignty remained predominantly national in many policy areas (Issing 2006). Due to this uniqueness, it is difficult to identify other banknotes that could truly serve as a basis for comparison.

According to the International Organization for Standardization, the euro is not alone in the class of 'supranational currencies'—also known as 'X currencies'.[2] All the other members, however, are currencies that refer to groups of former British or French colonies, such as the East Caribbean dollar, the African franc and the Pacific franc. The design of their banknotes reflects tensions associated with the process of decolonization rather than the struggle to achieve a common, supranational identity.

2 The International Organization for Standardization is responsible for a standard called *ISO 4217*, first published in 1978, which defines the designators of current and historic currencies.

For example, the East Caribbean dollar banknote, introduced in 1965, still features a portrait of Queen Elizabeth II on the obverse.

Looking for another term of comparison, one may be compelled to consider two countries whose paths towards unification were long and difficult and were ultimately able to bring together a multitude of heterogenous entities: Italy and Germany. The first banknote series of both the Italian lira and the German mark, issued in the 1860s and 1870s respectively, speaks a very similar language. In both cases, the newly established rulers used the banknotes as an opportunity to convey their own message, ignoring the diversity of the previous situation in favor of a singular representation of power. The designs were dominated by features such as portraits of the king and the kaiser, the armorial bearings of the House of Savoy and the German imperial crest and personifications of Italy and Germany in the form of female figures.

In the case of Germany, however, a different strategy was used for coins. In fact, all coins above one mark had a standard design for the reverse (the eagle insignia of the Reich), while each Land could choose its own design for the obverse, which usually consisted of a portrait of the local ruler or the city's coat of arms.

The distinction between obverse and reverse is significant because, more than one hundred years later, the same logic was applied to the euro coins. Unlike the banknotes, the coins have a multifaceted iconographic apparatus: they have a 'common side', which is the same in all countries, and a 'national side', which can be decided by each member state individually, provided that it respects the basic criteria defined by the European Monetary Institute (Raento 2004).

The decision to follow such an approach was taken at the Ecofin summit of April 1996 — the council of the economics and finance ministers of all European member states (CEC 2005). Several motivations were given to support national representation on euro coins, the main argument being that it could facilitate the transition toward a common currency in the eyes of many citizens. But there were also technical-juridical problems: for example, Belgium had a constitutional obligation to feature a portrait of the king on its coins.

Notwithstanding the opposition of both the European Monetary Institute and the European Commission, this two-sided scheme was eventually approved, after the ministers had accepted the compromise that the national designs would at least be framed by a circle with the twelve stars of the European flag. As noted by Oriane Calligaro, this compromise is emblematic of the constant tension between the two faces of European integration: the supranational side and the intergovernmental side (Calligaro 2013; Toemmel 2014). Unlike banknotes, coins had to be minted and issued by the national banks; therefore, they were partly under the jurisdiction of the member states.

As a result, one side of the euro coin varies from state to state. Several states chose to occupy this bastion of national pride with representations of architectural monuments. For example, Germany used the Brandenburg Gate on its 10-, 20- and 50-cent coins, Italy used the Colosseum on its 5-cent coin, and Austria used Olbrich's

Secession Building on its 50-cent coin. But there were also numerous portraits of 'great men', such as Mozart, Dante, Cervantes and several monarchs.

The specificity of these representations was in sharp contrast to the generic character of the common side, which featured a sequence of maps of Europe designed by Luc Luycx. A designer at the Belgian Royal Mint, Luycx made the case that 'a Europe-wide currency had to be neutral, the graphics could not be too specific; if I had opted for portraits of famous people or architectural monuments then one country was bound to be more strongly represented' (Luycx 2001).

The reiteration of traditional motifs in the only iconographic space that was still up to the states makes the direction taken by the European Monetary Institute with the banknotes seem even more ground-breaking. In Hymans's analysis, the fact that the euro banknotes were 'uninhabited' was associated with postmodernization and the turn against grand narratives and their heroes—a reading that aligned with a significant section of the discourse on European integration (Hymans 2004: 10; Van Ham 2001).[3] Notably, in the influential pamphlet *The Postmodern State*, published in the same year as the euro design competition, Robert Cooper described the European Union as 'the most developed example of a postmodern system' (Cooper 1996: 26).[4]

The final report of the Feature Selection Advisory Group reveals a certain reluctance to engage with the term 'modern'. In the aforementioned periodization for the euro banknotes, the final section started in the 1930s and was devoted to modern architecture (with a lower case 'm'). As evidenced by the report, the group 'discussed the modern or last banknote at length', and several members suggested 'that the modern period be replaced by another, previous period'. In the end, the group considered that, since the European Union and its institutions were conceived in the twentieth century, one banknote design had to represent this period (FSAG 1995: 9).

The concept of modernity is key because, historically, it underpinned the relationship between architecture and the state (Fig. 1). In the transatlantic context and beyond, the trajectory of modern architecture constantly paralleled that of the modern nation-state. Writing when architecture's association with the state was particularly strong, at the height of the Fascist regime in Italy, Giuseppe Terragni made the argument that 'architecture is a state art' (Terragni 1931). This declaration of interdependence spoke to a connection that had been crystallizing in Europe for more than three hundred years. Though its roots certainly go deeper, a point of reference can be identified in the seventeenth century, when the modern state system took form in Westphalia.

3 According to Hymans, two key aspects of the Euro banknotes 'push in a postmodern direction': the absence of human figures and the decision to obscure the 'original models there may have been for the depicted [architectural] structures'.

4 According to Cooper, there are several factors that distinguish postmodern systems from all others, including the blurring of the distinction between foreign and domestic affairs, the rejection of force for resolving disputes, the growing irrelevance of borders, voluntary mutual interference and surveillance.

Banknote number 7:

The architectural style: modern architecture
The period: from the 1930s onwards

Two leitmotifs of modern architecture are the adaptation of a building's form to its function (functionalism) and the attempt to gear the architecture to the needs of society. Representatives of functionalism endeavoured to bring individual expression into line with the requirements of functionalism, while the exponents of the Bauhaus style transferred anonymity - as a welcome manifestation of the industrial age - to architecture. In 1928 leading architects met for the first time at the International Congress of Modern Architecture (CIAM), founded by Le Corbusier and others. While no joint programme emerged, the Congress saw the crystallisation of a number of general demands which characterised the International Style: no ornamentation; flat roofs; straight contours; white, smoothly plastered walls; large windows.

Proposed design elements for banknote number 7

Proposal 1: Finlandia Hall in Helsinki.

Proposal 2: The Schroeder House in Utrecht.

6 Feature Selection Advisory Group, *Selection of Design Features for the European Banknote Series*, 1995. Introduction to the section on "modern architecture."
Source: Archives of the European Central Bank.

In this framework, architecture played a key role in the process of nation-building, while the state operated as the primary force and authority behind the production of architecture.

This balance of power started to change among the debris of World War II, accompanied by two dynamics that are rarely discussed together. On the one hand, the process of European integration led to forceful questioning and rescaling of statehood. The Treaty of Paris, the act that officially kickstarted this process in 1951, was an explicit attempt to move past the modern state system and its many problems, as the consequences of nationalism were still very much etched in everyone's memory.[5] In Cooper's analysis, a key aspect of this transition was a collective stance against the development of grandiose self-images (Foley 2007). On the other hand, what is known as the modern movement in architecture began to be radically challenged.

While most European states were transferring power to a new supranational system that political scientists defined as postmodern, those who heralded a postmodern turn in architecture failed to see the connection and, to this day, these two dis-

5 The process of European unification officially started in 1951 with the signing of the Paris Treaty, which established the European Coal and Steel Community between Belgium, France, Italy, Luxembourg, Netherlands and West Germany.

courses have not intersected. As an attempt to go beyond the modern nation-state, European integration was a process of both supranationalization and postmodernization. How did it engage with a discipline—architecture—that had been deeply entrenched in the very structures it aimed to overcome? In the area where European integration went the furthest, the area of monetary unification, architecture was immediately brought to the fore. The way the euro design competition was set up, however, shows that this embrace was accompanied not only by a resolute effort to cleanse architecture from its national liaisons, but also by an attempt to obscure the 'modern period' from the genealogy of European architecture.

History-Building: Copy, Cut, Paste, Delete

The set of guidelines, checks and balances defined in the preliminary stages of the euro project was ultimately intended to inform a selection of concrete examples that could appropriately represent the chosen 'ages and styles'. Although the operative goal was to put together a series of models that could serve as the basis for the required act of stylization, the by-product of this process was a more articulated document that shines a light on the difficulty of dislodging history-writing from nation-building.

Following the mandate of the European Monetary Institute, the Feature Selection Advisory Group ended up producing a two-part document—half text-based and half image-based. The former was attached to the final report under the bureaucratic label 'Annex 4' and comprised a description of the seven architectural styles. Each section included an introduction to the period at hand and a selection of representative buildings and features that are commonly associated with that style and ended with an overall explanation for those choices (FSAG 1995).

The descriptions focused on architectural types and elements. For example, the Classical period was associated with a selection of types (temple, aqueduct, theater etc.) and elements (column, base, entablature etc.) that could be easily abstracted from any specific building. In the areas that required specificity, namely the selection of representative examples, an effort was clearly made to pick buildings that were as politically correct as possible and conveyed the fewest nationalist messages.

In the chapter devoted to modern architecture, the advisors called into question the acceptability of most 'buildings in the Bauhaus style', which they associated with the failures of social housing in the *banlieues* of many European cities (Fig. 6). On the contrary, they thought that Alvar Aalto's Finlandia Hall was 'a most appropriate—albeit lesser known—symbol of European peace and unity', emphasizing the fact that the 1975 European Convention on Security and Cooperation had been signed in that building (FSAG 1995: 22).

Along with these writings, the feature group also assembled a selection of images that, according to the advisors, could represent the seven periods and styles. Unlike the textual descriptions, this 116-page document was later attached to the de-

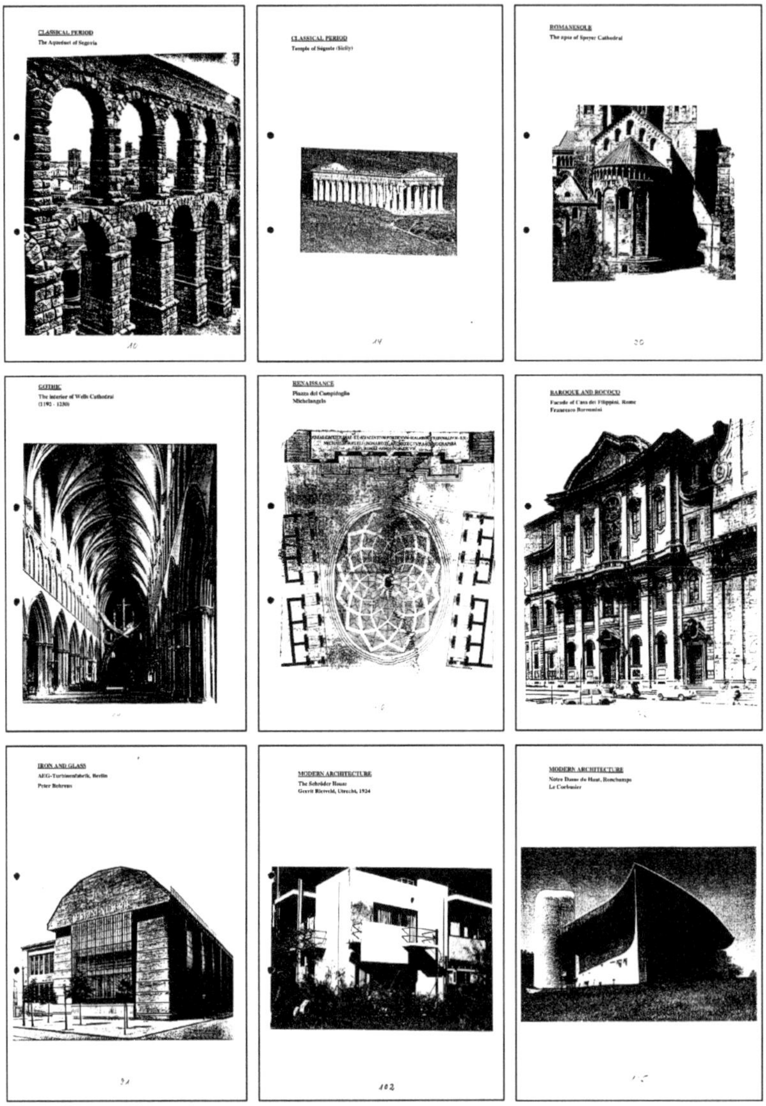

7 Feature Selection Advisory Group, *Selection of Design Features for the European Banknote Series*, 1995. Selection of nine pages of “primary architectural features” taken from the 116-page illustrated survey of European architecture produced by the FSAG.
Source: Archives of the European Central Bank.

sign competition brief, under the name ‘Appendix 2’ (Fig. 7–8). It consisted of a sequence of 108 black-and-white images of buildings, sculptures, paintings, drawings and photographs, ranging from the eighth century BC to the twentieth century (FSAG 1995).

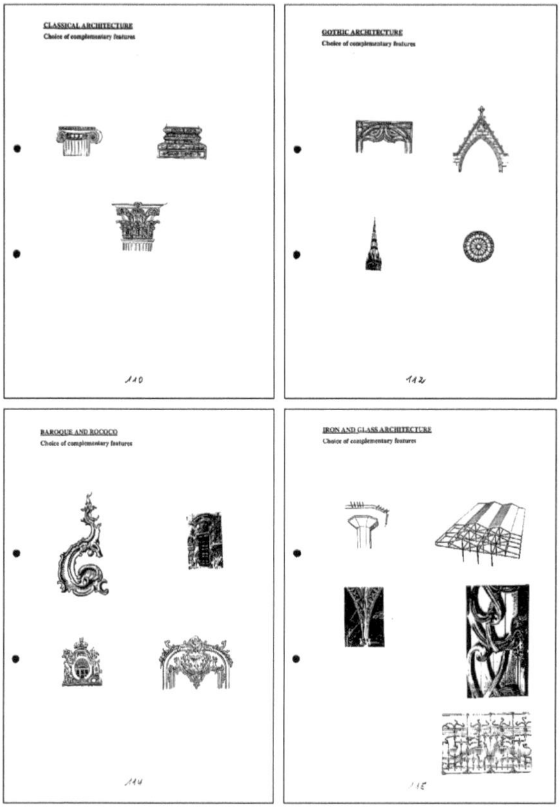

8 Feature Selection Advisory Group, *Selection of Design Features for the European Banknote Series*, 1995. Selection of four pages of "complementary architectural features" taken from the 116-page illustrated survey of European architecture produced by the FSAG.
Source: Archives of the European Central Bank.

In trying to understand how this document was constructed, two interviews, those with Jean-Michel Dinand, the executive of the European Monetary Institute who oversaw this process, and John Voncken, the architect who represented Luxembourg, were particularly important. As the only architect in these advisory groups, Voncken played a key role in the selection and definition of the final design. During our conversation, he recalled going to a meeting in Brussels after the competition and realizing that he was the only remaining counselor: 'From that moment on I became a little nervous ... I was in fact the only one to give the OK for all the banknote designs' (Voncken 2020).

According to Voncken, every member of the Feature Selection Advisory Group contributed to the construction of Appendix 2, although the three art historians (Jaap Bolten, Nicole Dacos Crifò and Aimo Reitala) took on a leading role. Dinand recalled that, at the first gathering in June 1995, everyone was asked to go through their own manuals of art and architectural history at home, select a series of images and make photocopies. At the following meeting at the Eurotower in Frankfurt, each photocopy was the object of a collective discussion: 'as a result of the *tour de table*, each image was either retained or discarded' (Dinand 2020). The janitor who emptied the trash bins of the EMI office that day must have been the only person who saw those discarded, alternative histories, made of features that were considered too nationally biased or politically incorrect.

No single book of art or architectural history can be identified as the predominant source for the selected images: they were taken from a multitude of books, as more than ten people pitched in and brought their own proposals. The images were cut and pasted onto A4 pages that had been previously set up with the corresponding captions and headers. Each page was then photocopied again to make it flat and run through a hole-puncher, so that it could be put in a binder. The manual labor that went into making this collage was performed by the staff of the Working Group on Printing and Issuing a European Banknote.

Although the art historians in the room were certainly used to working with slides, Voncken did not recall anyone handling or projecting slides during these meetings. The way Appendix 2 is structured, however, seems to align with the logic of the slideshow, which is based on the construction of a series of images, arranged in a linear progression and made homogeneous by a common standard framework (in this case, an A4 page).

But this document also had an operative character, in the sense that it was imagined as a concrete tool for the participants of a competition, who were asked to use these images as models for their own design proposals. One may be tempted to compare it to a model-book, a medium that goes back to the Middle Ages, when artists relied on compendiums of motifs passed from one generation to another, ready to be inserted into paintings and other artworks (Giles 2014). In the case of the euro design competition, however, the designers were not allowed to copy the assigned motifs and, instead, needed to 'stylize' them.

Overall, in an attempt to provide a system that could guide and channel the design of a new banknote series, the Feature Selection Advisory Group produced an illustrated survey of European art and architecture based on the logic of stylization, at a time when such an endeavor would have been widely regarded as anachronistic, to say the least. It was a history through images, made by many hands, informed by a multitude of ideological considerations and framed so as to discourage the reader from approaching it with a naïve or innocent eye (Gombrich 1960).[6] This body of images was explicitly presented to its intended audience (the participants of the competition) as material that was *guilty* of national bias and therefore needed to be transformed into something else.

A significant amount of naïveté, however, lay in the failure to recognize that, along with stylization, the production of history had also been entangled in the web of the nation-state. Since the nineteenth century, the construction of national styles had been accompanied by the writing of national histories: the two practices went hand in

6 With the expression 'innocent eye', Gombrich refers to the myth that images do not need to be read and that their reception does not depend on prior knowledge on the part of the beholder.

hand. As noted by Patrick Geary, 'the modern study of history was conceived and developed in the nineteenth century as an instrument of European nationalism' (Geary 2002: 15). Eric Hobsbawm put it more directly:

> Historians are to nationalism what poppy-growers in Pakistan are to the heroin-addicts: we supply the essential raw material for the market. Nations without a past are contradictions in terms. What makes a nation is the past, what justifies one nation against others is the past, and historians are the people who produce it. So, my profession, which has always been mixed up in politics, becomes an essential component of nationalism. (Hobsbawm 1992: 3).

In our case, the question is, how do historians relate to supranationalism? The easier option is to Photoshop the past, distorting it just enough to obscure its national connotations, while maintaining and taking full advantage of its aura. In essence, the task of the euro competition was to turn a history of buildings (Appendix 2) into a history without buildings, replacing images of specific objects with generic representations of style. The design of the euro was meant to draw from the past, but at the same time every site-specific—meaning, state-specific—reference had to be concealed. Getting rid of buildings was thought to be the most effective way of solving the problem of national bias. However, in addition to stylization, the very act of building historical narratives of this genre was itself deeply embedded in a conceptual framework of nation building, especially in Europe.

Design Selection: Negotiating the Public

In February 1996, shortly after the submission of the final report of the feature group, the euro design competition got under way. This marked a transition from setting up rules and choosing models to evaluating and ultimately selecting actual designs. The process was characterized by multiple, increasingly complex levels of evaluation, ranging from a jury panel to an opinion poll, from print and television media to the public at large.

The competition was not open to everyone: the European Monetary Institute asked each central bank to nominate a minimum of one and a maximum of three participants. In the end, twenty-nine participants (both individuals and teams) submitted proposals. While many of them were employees of the national banks, there were also nominees from the private sector (working for such well-connected companies as De La Rue Currency and Komori Currency Technology) and a few independent designers.[7]

7 In 2002, the European Central Bank organized and hosted an exhibition of all the designs submitted to the Euro competition. The catalog provides a great deal of information about the jury, the designers, their proposals and the entire competition process.

Meanwhile, the Working Group on Printing and Issuing a European Banknote assembled a jury of 'internationally renowned experts in marketing, design and art history', which met on 26 September 1996 to evaluate the proposals (ECB 2003: 8). The group included two art historians, along with jurors from the fields of graphic design, communications, marketing, advertising, broadcasting, curatorship, industrial design and psychology, many of whom came from academic institutions.

The task of the jury was to draw up a shortlist of ten proposals. Commenting on the decision of the jury, the chief cashier of the Bank of Finland Antti Heinonen (who later became director of banknotes at the European Central Bank) underlined the fact that 'there were few portraits in the various series it selected because even the slightest similarity to a real person could have been interpreted as favoritism towards a certain nationality' (Heinonen 2015: 62).

As soon as the jury had completed its work, the European Monetary Institute moved to the second, decisive phase of the evaluation process and hired EOS Gallup Europe (the overseas branch of Gallup, a major American analytics company specializing in opinion polls) to conduct a 'qualitative study' aimed at evaluating 'the reactions of the public and certain professionals who handle daily a large number of banknotes' to the shortlisted designs (EOSGE 1996: 2).[8]

Throughout October 1996, EOS Gallup Europe teamed up with multiple 'survey and research companies' in the countries that were expected to join the euro and interviewed almost 2,000 people. The findings were presented in a report sent to the European Monetary Institute on 6 December 1996 — a report taken very seriously by the Working Group on Printing and Issuing a European Banknote. In fact, the winner of the competition ended up being the proposal that performed best in Gallup's survey.

At a meeting in Frankfurt on 3 December 1996, having weighed the jury's evaluations and the survey results, the Council of the European Monetary Institute chose the proposal submitted by Robert Kalina, the banknote designer of Austria's national bank. A detail that is worth noting is that Kalina, in addition to working for the said bank, was also its nominee for both the theme group and the feature group, so he participated in the entire process leading up to the competition. Somehow this was not against the rules and none of the other designers complained.

An alumnus of the Hochschule für Graphische Künste in Vienna, Kalina began to work for the Austrian national bank in 1976 and designed all the Austrian schilling banknotes issued after 1982 (ECB 2003: 82–83). Notably, all his schilling designs were based on the 'masters and masterpieces' scheme. But Kalina's proposal for the euro banknotes went a different route. First, he was among the designers who fully embraced the architectural theme and did not include any human figures. Second, rather

8 Two recent exhibitions at the Canadian Centre for Architecture have touched on the impact of Gallup on Western politics and culture: *Architecture Itself and Other Postmodernist Myths* (2018) and *Our Happy Life: Architecture and Well-Being in the Age of Emotional Capitalism* (2019).

GALLUP EUROPE

EURO BANKNOTES TEST - FINAL REPORT - 6/12/1996 p. 25

2.2 Expressing a geographic link

Should the Euro notes absolutely give an impression of Europe or is it not necessary ? The question can remain unanswered as long as the notes avoid giving Europe a regional, limited or even national bias.

That is what we wanted to know by asking respondents if the notes evoked: the whole of Europe, only part of Europe, one country in particular or none of that ?

One might have feared that the "Ages and Styles" notes cause more problems than the others concerning regional or individual country bias. This effect was indeed felt but in an infinitely smaller way than we might have feared.

· 13. EUROPE CONVEYED.

(weighted : M.E.P.)	SETS :									
	A	B	C	D	E	F	G	H	I	K
BASIS : ALL INTERVIEWS	201 100%	193 100%	195 100%	183 100%	175 100%	202 100%	214 100%	183 100%	176 100%	174 100%
the whole of Europe	143 71%	146 76%	117 60%	96 52%	96 55%	86 42%	138 65%	110 60%	79 45%	50 29%
one region of Europe	21 10%	19 10%	25 13%	28 16%	23 13%	9 4%	6 3%	10 6%	12 7%	5 3%
one country in particular	26 13%	14 7%	28 14%	33 18%	22 13%	27 14%	20 9%	21 11%	29 16%	24 14%
neither Europe, nor region, nor country	12 6%	14 7%	25 13%	25 14%	34 19%	79 39%	49 23%	40 22%	54 31%	92 53%
(d.k./n.a.)			1 0%			1 1%	1 1%	1 1%	1 1%	3 2%

9 EOS Gallup Europe, *Euro Banknotes Test Results and Comments*, 1996. This part of Gallup's evaluation was aimed at finding the least nationally biased design. Kalina's winning proposal is "set B."
Source: Archives of the European Central Bank.

than engaging with buildings, he elected to focus on what he called 'architectural elements' — an approach that recalls Rem Koolhaas's project at the 2014 Venice Biennale. Kalina's idea was to display windows and gateways on the front of the banknotes and bridges on the back — three elements that were meant to symbolize openness, cooperation and communication. Along with stylization, this elemental approach was instrumental in isolating architecture from its historical and geographical bonds, which would have contradicted the supranational ambition of the project. As noted by Koolhaas, the fundamental elements of architecture can be 'used by any architect, anywhere, anytime'. Such breakdown then opens the possibility to 'reconstruct the global history of each element' (Koolhaas 2004).

The data gathered by EOS Gallup Europe played a key role in the selection process. When asked what Kalina's banknotes 'talked about', 84 % of the interviewees pointed to architecture. More than 60 % of them found his design 'attractive' or 'very attractive' and said that it inspired confidence. The survey also endeavored to test the performance of each proposal vis-à-vis a series of binary attributes. Kalina's proposal proved the best balance between 'unity and diversity' and between 'past and future' in the representation of European identity. It also tested well in the section that evaluated the gender connotation of the banknotes: the interviewees thought it had perfect balance between femininity and masculinity. The key question, however, had to do with national bias (Fig. 9). Kalina's entry was perceived as the most supranational, since more than three-fourths of the people said that it did not favor any one country or region; instead, it evoked 'the whole of Europe' (EOSGE 1996).

Nevertheless, shortly after the European Monetary Institute had presented the winning proposal to the public at a press conference on 13 December 1996, the issue of national bias came up again. After a few weeks, Russ Swan, the editor of the British magazine *Bridge Design and Engineering*, conducted a thorough investigation into Kalina's banknotes and was able to point out a number of similarities between his designs and real bridges.

Swan was invited to talk about it on BBC's *Newsnight* and the story was quickly picked up and disseminated by a multitude of media outlets throughout the world. In his BBC interview, Swan was accompanied to the stage by the soundtrack of *Mission Impossible* (the chairman of the European Monetary Institute had said that it would be impossible to identify the bridges) and presented his case in front of exhibit boards with enlargements of the euro banknotes, mimicking the dynamics of a trial or, perhaps more appropriately, a legal drama. In his presentation, Swan argued that some of Kalina's bridges did not meet the requirement of being devoid of identifiable characteristics, because he could spot details copied from the Pont de Neuilly in Paris, the Rialto in Venice and other well-known bridges (Swan 2010).

Under public pressure, the European Monetary Institute had to ask Kalina to modify his designs to make them less recognizable and more generic. The Working Group on Printing and Issuing a European Banknote tried to put together yet another group of 'experts' to oversee this process (Heinone 2015: 91–92). Voncken was the only one who agreed to take on this unique architectural consultancy. Like many other members of the feature group, Voncken had thought that Kalina's 'invented architecture' would raise a lot of eyebrows: as it turned out, the problem was that it was not *invented* enough (Voncken 2020). In a later interview with *The Wall Street Journal* about the redesign of his bridges, Kalina noted: 'I thought I had changed them enough the first time; apparently, I didn't' (Steinmetz 1998).

As highlighted in an article published by *City Lab*, the redesign process was facilitated by the fact that Kalina, like Luc Luycx and many of the other designers involved in the euro competition, did not elaborate his proposal by hand: 'He was inspired by specific bridges and used a computer to combine various real-world components so as to obscure their initial identities' (Grabar 2013). Kalina actually publicized

10–11 Robert Kalina and Luc Luyxc, 1997. These almost identical, staged photographs of Kalina, the designer of the Euro banknotes (left) and Luyxc, the designer of the common side of the Euro coins (right) speak to the importance that was attributed to the use of computers.
Source: Archives of the European Central Bank and Numismag.

his preference for digital technologies. Most of the newspaper articles on this topic were accompanied by a staged photograph of Kalina in his office, posing in front of two computer monitors with images of his banknotes (Figs. 10–11).

The question of technology is key. Perhaps unknowingly, the action that the European Monetary Institute asked the participating designers to perform was precisely that which raster graphics software such as Photoshop had just been created to accomplish. Firstly, the entire process revolved around bi-dimensional images. More importantly, the task was to manipulate these images and, through a process of stylization, generate an original representation of elements that did not exist but looked recognizable and realistic. As illustrated by Amy Kulper, the fundamental operation of digital tools like Photoshop is to move us away from the object, while giving us the impression of moving closer to the realism of the object. The images produced by Kalina were designed to resemble a Classical aqueduct or a Gothic window (Fig. 12). But, in fact, they resulted from a 'critical move away from the object' — our (nationally biased) history of architecture — that was facilitated and magnified by the digital turn (Kulper 2016).

While Kalina had to go 'back to his computer' and adjust his banknotes, the European Monetary Institute took the opportunity to look for other possible issues and, to avoid any other controversy, went so far as to hire an engineer to check the structural soundness of his designs (Steinmetz 1998). Since it is generally important for a currency to project strength and stability, the Working Group on Printing and Issuing a European Banknote wanted to make sure that these bridges would not collapse if they were built.

12 European Central Bank, *Euro Banknote Design Exhibition*, 2003. Kalina's final design as illustrated in the catalogue of the exhibition organized by the ECB to showcase the results of the Euro competition. Source: Archives of the European Central Bank.

Building the Euro: Architecture as Nation-Unbuilding

In a bizarre twist of life imitating art, the Dutch artist Robin Stam took up the challenge and, right after the euro crisis of 2009, launched a project called *The Bridges of Europe* in the town of Spijkenisse, near Rotterdam. Almost ten years after the new banknotes had entered the wallets of more than three hundred million Europeans, this project gave an additional dimension to the struggle of bending architecture in a supranational direction, turning Kalina's images into models for concrete buildings (Fig. 14).

Stam's idea was to expose the logic behind the design of the euro banknotes: 'Wouldn't it be amazing if these fictional bridges suddenly turn out to exist in real life?' (Stam 2011). In 2011, he pitched his idea to a friend in the city council of Spijkenisse, which had just started building a middle-class housing development on the outskirts of town. As is customary in the Netherlands, the site was surrounded by canals and therefore required several bridges for pedestrian and bicycle crossings. The city council saw it as a good way to promote the new development and decided to fund Stam's bridges, even though they were 25 % more expensive than the catalog bridges that were initially intended for the site.

In his own writings and interviews, Stam kept framing this act of retro-construction as something funny, hilarious, ironic (Griffiths 2013). In the end, his 'joke' cost about one million euros. For the head of the city council, however, 'all the attention was more than worth it' (Grabar 2013). One of the ironic aspects of this project was that the reproductions of the 'grandiose looking' bridges on the banknotes were built over narrow canals. Even though they were blow-ups of pocket-size images, they still looked awkwardly small in comparison to the height of a person or a bicycle.

To enhance the effect of the project, the bridges needed to be exact replicas of Kalina's designs, down to the color and the most inconspicuous details. For example, Stam elected to crop the edges of his little structures, because they were not visible on the bills. Overall, the bridges were built by pouring colored concrete into finely decorated wooden molds with relief patterns that gave the impression of stone or brick, except for the last two bridges, the 'modern' ones, which had to be built out of steel (Fig. 13).

While the design of the euro had revolved around the idea of erasing buildings and transcending architecture into the realm of historically allusive images — an idea that aligned with one of the founding myths of postmodernism — Stam's project aimed to turn the tables and, albeit with a (postmodernist) act of irony, put buildings back at the center of this process.[9]

It is worth noting that Stam is a graphic designer and, much like Kalina, has no background in architecture or engineering. Hence, unknowingly following in the footsteps of the European Monetary Institute, he assembled a 'team of experts' to help him put his idea into action (Grabar 2013). Remarkably, in a story that revolved around architecture, the protagonists had little or no knowledge of architecture.

At the core of Stam's project was an interest in exposing Europe's struggle to deal with different and opposing national identities. He referred to the euro banknotes as 'member-state-neutral' objects, which was why they had to be 'fictional' (Stam 2011). One of the outcomes of his project was that, after the transition from fiction to fact, all the bridges ended up existing in only one country, the Netherlands. Playing with this contradiction, Stam went so far as to raise the issue with the European Central Bank, which proved to have a sense of humor and replied with an official letter of approval (Allen 2011).

Discussing the difficulties of creating the euro, the head of the Deutsche Bundesbank's Money Museum, Heike Winter, pointed out that until then banknote design had been inseparably linked with national self-image (Winter 2004). As money was seen as a means for states to construct simple messages through images and immediately have them reach the pockets of millions of people, architectural representations associated with (more or less) fictional histories of those states were often at the center of this communication.

Much has been written about the relationship between architecture and nation-building. There is also a vast literature on the role that architectural history played in this process. In his book *European Architecture 1750–1890*, Barry Bergdoll addresses the remarkable case of the cornerstone ceremony for Soufflot's church of Ste-Geneviève, orchestrated by Louis XV in 1764: 'The cornerstone contained a copy of

9 Sylvia Lavin, *Building Postmodernism*, doctoral seminar at UCLA, Winter 2015. Lavin challenges the notion that postmodern architecture is about image culture and, instead, focuses on buildings — 'the one thing postmodernity, theoretically, could not produce'.

13–14 Robin Stam, *The Bridges of Europe*, 2011. Construction of the 200-Euro, 19th century bridge (top) and the 5-Euro, classical bridge (bottom) in the Spijkenisse housing development.
Source: Robin Stam.

Leroy's *History of the Form and Layout which the Christians have given their Temples from Constantine to our own Time*; an Enlightenment philosophy of history literally became the cornerstone of the new building' (Bergdoll 2001: 29–30). While the young French state relied on architecture to produce grandiose representations of its powers, it also recognized the effect of presenting the said architecture as the latest (and greatest) development in a long historical progression, which embraced and appropriated a multitude of cultures. The role of Leroy's genealogical tree of architectural plans was

3. Identification of architectural features

The report of the Theme Selection Advisory Group describes the inclusion of architecture in the theme "Ages and Styles" as 'an artist's representation of the architectural style of the period (e.g. classical, Gothic, Renaissance, baroque, neoclassical, etc.). This side of the note would thus convey, without specific reference to any given building, a clear message on the architectural richness and unity of Europe'.

The series of features selected in proposals 1 and 2 with a view to minimising national bias could represent the architectural styles enumerated in paragraph 2. Some additional features have been suggested for considation as alternatives.

	Proposal 1	Proposal 2	Alternatives
Classical	The Maison Carrée in Nîmes	Pont du Gard (Roman aqueduct)	a) An original Greek temple b) The aqueduct at Segovia
Romanesque	The apse from Lund Cathedral	A series of arches inside the Abbey of Mont-Saint-Michel	a) The apse from Speyer Cathedral
Gothic	The interior of Wells cathedral	The frontal view of portals of Amiens Cathedral	-

15 Feature Selection Advisory Group, *Selection of Design Features for the European Banknote Series*, 1995.
Source: Archives of the European Central Bank.

to elevate both Soufflot's building and, more importantly, the seat of power that commissioned it, by giving them a historical mission.

But how do architecture and architectural history relate to the process of nation-unbuilding in Europe and the emergence of a system that, since the early 1950s, has aimed to go beyond the realm of the state? Although the architectural discourse is often accused of being too Eurocentric and too politicized, we have mostly ignored the political dynamic that, more than any other, has been transforming the European archipelago over the past seventy years: the process of European unification.

In the area of monetary unification, the area in which Europe reached its highest level of integration, architecture was recognized as the most appropriate tool for the construction of a supranational message. However, the architectural imagery of the euro banknotes had to cope with the paradoxical condition of needing to be 'nation neutral' and, at the same time, embedded in a historical narrative that would inevitably intersect with national dynamics (Fig. 15).

A history was needed to provide concrete models and, above all, an overarching system that would help situate fictional architecture in real time, making it seem legible and legitimate. But, except for the small group of designers and bank executives involved in the process, no one could see the materials of this history, as they would have given away the national underpinnings of this supposedly supranational endeavor.

Perhaps that is why, instead of being celebrated in the *place publique* like Leroy's work, the document produced by the Feature Selection Advisory Group was marked as confidential and hidden in the archive of the European Central Bank. Not only is history as a medium embedded in the episteme of the modern nation-state, but also its content is mostly made of objects with some level of national connotation. In the postmodern, supranational order to which the European Union aspires, how can a history of architecture pass the test of political correctness?

References

Allen, K. 2011. An Uncommon Monument to the Common Currency. *Spiegel International* (online), 4 November. Available at https://www.spiegel.de/international/zeitgeist/euro-bridges-an-uncommon-monument-to-the-common-currency-a-795930.html [Last accessed 1 December 2020].

Bergdoll, B. 2001. *European Architecture, 1750–1890*. Oxford: Oxford University Press.

Calligaro, O. 2013. *Negotiating Europe*. New York: Palgrave Macmillan.

CEC [Commission of the European Communities]. 2005. Recommendation on Common Guidelines for the National Side of Euro Circulation Coins. *Official Journal of the European Union*. Available at https://eur-lex.europa.eu/eli/reco/2005/491/oj [Last accessed 1 December 2020].

Chang, M. 2009. *Monetary Integration in the European Union*. New York: Palgrave Macmillan.

Choay, F. 2001. *The Invention of the Historic Monument*. Cambridge: Cambridge University Press.

Cooper, R. 1996. *The Postmodern State and the World Order*. London: Demos.

Dinand, J. 2020. Interview by Sebastiano Fabbrini, 2 March.

ECB [European Central Bank]. 2003. *Euro Banknote Design Exhibition*. Frankfurt: European Central Bank.

EMI [European Monetary Institute]. 1996. *Design Brief for the Design of a Series of Euro Banknotes*. ECB Archives.

EOSGE [European Omnibus Survey Gallup Europe]. 1996. *Final Report: Euro Banknotes Test Results and Comments*. ECB Archives.

Foley, F. 2007. *Between Force and Legitimacy: The Worldview of Robert Cooper*. Florence: European University Institute.

FSAG [Feature Selection Advisory Group]. 1995. *Selection of Design Features: Report of the Feature Selection Advisory Group to the European Monetary Institute's Working Group on Printing and Issuing a European Banknote*. ECB Archives.

Geary, P. 2002. *The Myth of Nations: The Medieval Origins of Europe*. Princeton: Princeton University Press.

Giles, L. (ed.) 2014. *Italian Master Drawings from the Princeton University Art Museum*. Princeton: Princeton University Art Museum.

Gombrich, E. 1960. *Art and Illusion: A Study in the Psychology of Pictorial Representation*. Princeton: Princeton University Press.

Grabar, H. 2013. Europe's Most Famous Fictional Bridges, Brought to Life. *City Lab* (online), 14 June. Available at https://www.bloomberg.com/news/articles/2013-06-14/europe-s-most-famous-fictional-bridges-brought-to-life [Last accessed 1 December 2020].

Griffiths, A. 2013. Fictional Bridges on Euro Banknotes Constructed in the Netherlands. *Dezeen* (online), 5 June. Available at https://www.dezeen.com/2013/06/05/the-bridges-of-europe-robin-stam-copied-from-euro-banknotes/ [Last accessed 1 December 2020].

Harloe, K. 2013. *Winckelmann and the Invention of Art History*. Oxford: Oxford University Press.

Heinonen, A. 2015. *The First Euros*. Frankfurt: European Central Bank.

Hobsbawm, E. 1992. Ethnicity and Nationalism in Europe Today. *Anthropology Today*, 8(1): 3–8.

Hobsbawm, E. and Ranger, T. (eds.). 1993. *The Invention of Tradition*. Cambridge: Cambridge University Press.

Hübsch, H. 1992. *In What Style Should We Build? The German Debate on Architectural Style* [1828]. Trans. by W. Herrmann. Santa Monica: Getty Publications.

Hymans, J. 2004. The Changing Color of Money: European Currency Iconography and Collective Identity. *European Journal of International Relations*, 10(1): 5–31.

Issing, O. 2006. *The Euro: A Currency without a State*. Public speech, Helsinki, 24 March. Available at https://www.ecb.europa.eu/press/key/date/2006/html/sp060324.en.html [Last accessed 1 December 2020].

Koolhaas, R. 2014. *Elements of Architecture*. Milan: Taschen.

Kulper, A. 2016. *Architecture's Digital Turn and the Advent of Photoshop*. Lecture at the Canadian Centre for Architecture, 9 June. Available at https://www.cca.qc.ca/en/articles/issues/4/origins-of-the-digital/41052/architectures-digital-turn-and-the-advent-of-photoshop [Last accessed 1 December 2020].

Lavin, S. 2020. *Architecture Itself and Other Postmodernization Effects*. Leipzig: Spector Books.

Luycx, L. 2001. Ready to Jangle Some New Loose Change? *Deutsche Welle*, 25 December.

Mulhearn, C. and Vane, H. 2008. *The Euro: Its Origins, Development and Prospects*. Cheltenham: Edward Elgar.

Raento, P. et al. 2004. Striking Stories: A Political Geography of Euro Coinage. *Political Geography*, 23(8): 929–956.

Stam, R. 2011. *The Bridges of Europe*. Tumblr. Available at https://thebridgesofeurope.tumblr.com/ [Last accessed 1 December 2020].

Steinmetz, G. 1998. The Euro Designer's Art Will Have a Wide Currency. *The Wall Street Journal*, 7 July, p. B1.

Swan, R. 2010. *The Euro*. Blog. Available at http://russswan.com/about/the-euro/ [Last accessed 1 December 2020].

Terragni, G. 1931. Architettura di Stato. *L'Ambrosiano*, 11 February.

Toemmel, I. 2014. *The European Union: What It Is and How It Works*. New York: Palgrave Macmillan.

TSAG [Theme Selection Advisory Group]. 1995. *Interim Report to the European Monetary Institute's Working Group on Printing and Issuing a European Banknote on the Selection of a Theme for the European Banknote Series*. ECB Archives.

Van Ham, P. 2001. *European Integration and the Postmodern Condition: Governance, Democracy, Identity*. New York: Routledge.

Voncken, J. 2020. Interview by Sebastiano Fabbrini, 16 January.

Winter, H. 2004. *The Design of Euro Banknotes*. In: Proceedings of the 11th Meeting of the International Committee of Money and Banking Museums, Seoul.

Chapter 6
Fragmentation and Integration: Stairway to Europe

Abstract

This chapter sets out to explore the transformative effects of European funding on architecture. The case study is the public escalator of Toledo, a project that exposes how the European Union, in addition to and in exchange for its financial backing, indirectly reshapes both the content and the method of design, creating a complex system of incentives and rewards. At the heart of this process is a fragmentation of the structures of power that have historically disciplined the field.

The Exhibition/Spanishness at the MoMA

On February 12, 2006, the exhibition *On-Site: New Architecture in Spain* opened at the Museum of Modern Art, in New York City (Fig. 1). The show put on display fifty-three projects that, in the words of the curator Terence Riley, "illustrate why Spain is increasingly known as the home of some of architecture's most innovative voices, who are creating new works of the highest design ambition, many unfolding right before our eyes." The underlying thesis of the exhibition, however, was that the emergence of this new *school* of architecture had been made possible by Spain's entry into the European Communities (which had meanwhile coalesced into the European Union) and, more specifically, by the ensuing influx of huge amounts of European funds. Notably, the show was organized on the twentieth anniversary of Spain joining the European Union. Over that twenty-year period, Spain had been the largest net receiver of any EU member, taking nearly $ 110 billion in funding for projects in the built environment, including many of the projects on display at MoMA.

The central principle of the EU's cohesion policy is to financially support the less developed regions in order to align standards of living across the continent. When Spain became a member, it had been a democracy for less than ten years (not counting the failed military coup of 1981) and, before that, had experienced thirty-six years of dictatorship under Francisco Franco. The entire country fell under "objective 1" of European regional development, which indicated the need for "structural adjustments."

1 Entrance to the MoMA exhibition On-Site: New Architecture in Spain.
New York, 2006.
Source: MoMA.

While acknowledging that the Spanish projects on display needed to be viewed through the lens of European integration, the MoMA exhibition did not question the impact of that process on architecture beyond the financial level. In the catalogue, Riley made the case that, although most of the projects had been paid for by the European Union, they did not constitute "some undistinguishable Euro-architecture" and instead showed a distinctive Spanishness.

On one hand, for all its idiosyncrasies, the European Union is not unlike any other large, powerful organization when it comes to financing, in the sense that the dispensing of funds is always accompanied by precise requirements. In fact, this is how the engine of European integration works — it provides economic support in exchange for reforms that are in line with a common agenda. On the other hand, this engine makes very little noise: political scientists refer to it as "hidden integration" or "integration by stealth," alluding to the fact that the transformative effects of this process are rarely publicized and, instead, need to be read between the lines.

Looking back at the architectural discourse of the 1990s and the early 2000s, it was as if none of this was happening. Especially in Europe. It was quite emblematic that the first major event to touch on the relation between architecture and European integration, albeit in a limited manner, took place at the MoMA, on the other side of the Atlantic. At least Riley was willing to recognize that there was something bigger behind the new wave of Spanish architects emerging in the 1990s. Due to its supercharged integration over a short period of time, Spain was indeed an ideal case to shine light on these dynamics. Funding was one part of it, but what about the counterpart, the process we may call *integrating architecture*, meaning the discrete yet impactful hand that the European Union laid on architecture?

The Agreement/Toledo and the European Agenda

Of all the projects displayed at the MoMA, the last one, which concluded the exhibition, coalesced these tensions in a particularly palpable way. Presented as *La Granja Escalators*, it consisted of a series of moving staircases designed by Catalan architects José Antonio Martínez Lapeña and Elías Torres Tur, connecting a new parking lot to the historical center of Toledo. It all started on July 23, 1997, when the City Council of Toledo signed a *convenio* (agreement) with the European Investment Bank (EIB), the financing arm of the European Union, which made available 3,800,000,000 pesetas for a project of *renovación urbana* (Fig. 2).

As I began gathering materials and information from archives and relevant stakeholders, I quickly realized that this stairway could be read as a significant example of how deep and multifaceted the influence of European integration can be. Upon reading the contract agreement, the first aspect that stood out concerned the governance of architecture. The deal was signed by the mayor of Toledo and the director of the European Investment Bank, while the role of the Spanish government was limited to giving a mark of approval, blessing the marriage between *el banco* and *el beneficiario*.

In the area of cohesion policy, the European Union interacts with and supports projects proposed by regional (or sub-regional) authorities, not national governments. The process of integration is tied to a fragmented conception of the member states, as the money flows on a supranational-to-regional axis, bypassing the national level. Since the early days of the community, the idea of the European Commission was to reduce the power of the states by pursuing the vision of a "Europe of the regions"—a multitude of territorial fragments, ideally with a cross-border dimension.

These dynamics cannot be understated, considering the degree to which architecture had been historically entrenched in the policies and the structures of the state. While this was true in most European countries, Spain was an extreme example of the symbiosis between architecture and the state: until the mid-1970s, it was ruled by a regime that regarded architecture as a state art and used it, rather explicitly, as an instrument to pursue its nationalist agenda. For Francisco Franco, architecture was "the alphabet of kings."

One of the requirements set by the European Investment Bank was that the *Ayuntamiento* (City Council) of Toledo did not manage the project of urban renewal directly, but rather empowered a specialized agency, that needed to have a *naturaleza mercantil* ("commercial nature") and a high degree of autonomy from local politics. Furthermore, the bank stipulated that the development and implementation of the project had to go through a competitive bidding process: every competition needed to be transparent, open to all members of the European Economic Area and compliant with EU directives.

The production of architecture was therefore shifted not only from the national level to the regional or local level, but also from the closed sphere of politics to

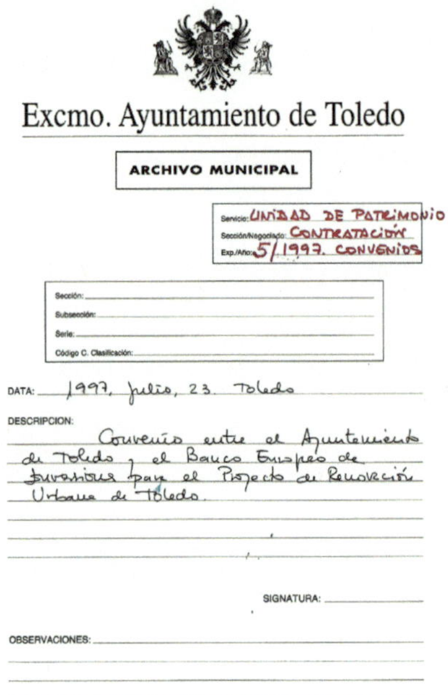

Excmo. Ayuntamiento de Toledo

ARCHIVO MUNICIPAL

Servicio: UNIDAD DE PATRIMONIO
Sección/Negociado: CONTRATACIÓN
Exp./Año: 5/1997. CONVENIOS

Sección:
Subsección:
Serie:
Código C. Clasificación:

DATA: 1997, julio, 23. Toledo

DESCRIPCION: Convenio entre el Ayuntamiento de Toledo y el Banco Europeo de Inversiones para el Proyecto de Renovación Urbana de Toledo.

SIGNATURA:

OBSERVACIONES:

2 Cover of the agreement (convenio) between the City Council of Toledo and the European Investment Bank, July 23, 1997.
Source: Archivio Municipal de Toledo.

the open sphere of the market. As noted by the EU Policy Lab, one of the underlying goals of European policymaking is to incentivize a change and homogenization of practices and modes of conduct, especially in the smaller, less developed regions. Toledo is a case in point. After the collaboration with the European Investment Bank, the City Council continued to hold open competitions based on EU rules and kept relying on that independent agency (called EMV) to oversee its interventions in the built environment.

Moreover, fifteen years after the success of *La Granja Escalators*, a second, very similar escalator was built on the other side of the Toledo citadel, following in the footsteps of the project by Martínez Lapeña & Torres. This time, however, the entire undertaking was promoted and financed by the Junta de Comunidades, the regional government of Castilla- La Mancha, showing how the input of the European Union had been completely assimilated in terms of both content and method.

Speaking of content, the European Investment Bank has always been very selective about the type of project it supports, looking for proposals that are in keeping with its agenda. Greg Clark has pointed out that the bank began to outline a "city agenda" in 1988, precisely as a way to cope with the 1986 enlargement that had brought the entire Iberian Peninsula into the European Community. Since then, this agenda has changed and evolved with the times. Over the past decade, for example, it has been focusing on environmental sustainability: good luck getting a project funded if it is not "green."

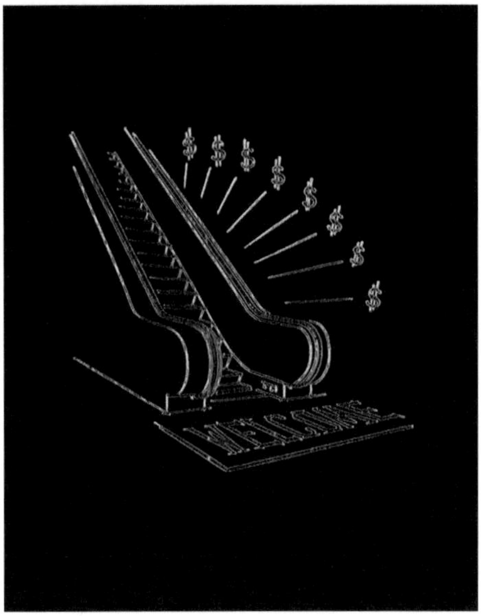

3 Escalator on the cover of Rem Koolhaas's the Harvard Guide to Shopping, 2001.
Source: OMA, elaboration from an Otis Elevator Co. Brochure.

Back in the 1990s, however, it focused on "urban renewal" with an emphasis on two key issues: transport and heritage. The European Investment Bank made an important step forward in formalizing its agenda in 1997, immediately before the Toledo agreement, when it published the so-called "Amsterdam Special Action Program," which defined guidelines and priorities for European investments. In the area of urban renewal, the program was centered on the upgrading of historical centers and the improvement of urban transport. Presented as a moving staircase that could reduce traffic and make the most of the historical heritage of the old city, the Toledo project seemed tailored to meet these criteria.

The Escalator/Modernization and Commodification

The escalator had a talismanic role. Since its inception, one of the core principles of the European Investment Bank has been to promote the modernization of the continent's less developed regions. Throughout its history, dating back to the nineteenth century, the escalator was constantly presented and perceived as a symbol of modernity—its seamless, mechanized movement representing, in a rather theatrical way, the pursuit of technological progress.

Looking at this history, however, it is also clear that the escalator has been inextricably linked to a specific activity: shopping. As noted by Rem Koolhaas, the escalator was the element that effectively enabled the development of department stores, transforming virtual space (the levels above the ground floor) into retail area (Fig. 3). After being exhibited as a new technological wonder—somewhat of a magic trick—at the world's fairs of the turn of the century, the escalator was almost exclusively employed in department stores, from Bon Marché to Bloomingdale's. At the heart of this application was the idea that maximum circulation equaled maximum sales volume. This principle was subsequently embraced in other places concerned with allowing large numbers of people to move through them and consume their content, especially cultural institutions. The escalator running through the façade of the Centre Pompidou exemplifies this transition.

In the case of Toledo, the vision behind the stairway was tied to the ambition of turning the city into a tourist destination. Before pitching the idea of the *escalera mecánica* to the European Investment Bank, the mayor of Toledo and three other members of the City Council went on a trip to Italy to visit the public escalators of Perugia and the public elevators of Urbino — two cities that had already built vertical, mechanical systems to connect their historical centers to lower, parking hubs. They returned home convinced that the escalator was a much better option. In fact, these two technologies have quite different effects on the city and its experience. The elevator produces division, blindly transporting people from point A to point B. It works well in office buildings or residential complexes, where the goal is to get to the point as quickly as possible. But it is not suited to environments where people are invited to stroll without a clear goal, spend as much time as possible and, to quote Roland Barthes, fulfil the modern desire to see and to be seen.

In the description of their project, Martínez Lapeña & Torres explained that the whole town of Toledo was approached as if it were a large building, and the escalator was imagined as the new defining element of its façade. Escalators have a unique ability to generate unity out of fragmentation, turning a multitude of separate spaces into a coherent structure. When used at the scale of the city, they turn heterogeneous urban fragments into a cohesive, continuous edifice that no longer responds to the logic of urban design, but rather to that of architecture.

In 1992, Michael Sorkin's influential book *Variations on a Theme Park* came out. Reworking a collage by Jacques Prévert entitled *The Pleasures of Progress*, the cover featured a group of costumed characters that appeared to have been taken out of a Renaissance painting and placed within a large, Piranesian shopping mall, climbing an escalator. Although the book focused primarily on American dynamics, the escalator was presented as a universal symbol for the process of theming and, consequently, commodification of the built environment.

Of course, the escalator designed by Martínez Lapeña & Torres did not turn Toledo into a theme park or a shopping mall. However, in that place and time, it was the type of intervention that, especially in the eyes of an institution like the European Investment Bank, pressed the right buttons and signaled a clear intention. It helped present a vision of the city as a homogeneous object with a prevailing function: tourism. In the framework of the EU's cohesion policy, every project is evaluated on the basis of its possible economic impact. The *escalera mecánica* represented a convincing indicator that the European investment had a good chance to pay off.

4 Logo of the European Union Prize for Contemporary Architecture. Source: European Commission.

The Award/Hidden Patronage

From this perspective, European integration can be said to have an indirect impact on the built environment. The EU obviously does not have the power to directly intervene in reshaping Toledo or any other site — until the Maastricht Treaty, the Community institutions did not even have the legal authority to shape their own headquarters. No one is forced to comply with its agenda, but those who diverge are very unlikely to receive funding. In other areas, for example as it pertains to building standards, the impact is much more direct: in the early 2000s, all member states were required, via directives, to replace their national building codes with Eurocodes. The European structural and investment funds, on the other hand, are based on a system of incentives and rewards.

One of the aspects that contribute to the relevance of the Toledo project is the fact that, shortly after its completion, it was selected for the 2001 European Union Prize for Contemporary Architecture, also known as the Mies van der Rohe Award. The prize was established in 1987 by the European Commission and the European Parliament in collaboration with the Mies van der Rohe Foundation in Barcelona. It was promoted by Carlo Ripa di Meana, who at the time was serving as the European Commissioner for Culture and the Environment. This initiative started less than one year after Spain had joined the European Communities and Mies's Barcelona pavilion had been reconstructed. As stated by the organizers, the goal of the award is to "highlight the involvement of the European Union in supporting architecture as an important element that reflects both the diversity of European architectural expression and its role as a unifying element to define a common European culture" (Fig. 4).

The building that, to quote Luis Fernández-Galiano, marked Spain's entrance into modernity reappeared precisely as Spain was entering the European Communities. After the demolition of Mies's 1929 pavilion, and for most of Franco's regime, modern architecture was actually banned by the Spanish state. Even though, by the 1980s, architecture had moved in a very different direction, the impetus to rebuild this highly symbolic structure was aimed at indicating a concrete connection between Barcelona, the trajectory of modernity and international dynamics. The Mies van der Rohe Foundation was established in 1983 by the City Council of Barcelona to oversee this difficult operation.

5 At the 2014 Venice Biennale, the Mies van der Rohe Foundation, and the European Commission organized an exhibition titled *Made in Europe*, putting on display 25 years of the European Union Prize for Contemporary Architecture.
Source: European Commission.

For the Community institutions, sponsoring an award dedicated to Mies, an architect who was forced to flee Europe and spent thirty years in the United States (becoming an American citizen), was a highly symbolic act too. The force that pushed Mies to leave Germany in the 1930s was the very force that European integration was built to leave behind: nationalism.

On a biennial basis, the Mies van der Rohe Award has been elevating a limited number of projects that are thought to represent "excellence in European architecture in conceptual, social, cultural, technical and constructive terms." Notably, two organizations are involved in the selection that also contribute to the effort of *integrating architecture*: the Architects' Council of Europe and the European Association for Architectural Education — two Brussels-based associations that have been trying to promote a European coordination of both the professional and the educational sides of architecture. The winners receive a cash prize, funded by the European Union, and a little "sculpture" of Mies's pavilion. The awards ceremony, held in Barcelona and chaired by representatives of EU institutions, is always followed by the publication of a catalogue and a traveling exhibition, with the aim of showcasing what are "best practices" throughout the continent (Fig. 5).

The opening sentence of the jury citation for the Toledo project read as follows: "The historical centers of many cities face the problem of compatibility between vehicular and pedestrian circulation; in Toledo, the first great steps have been taken to solve the difficulties of accessibility to the old part of the city." Heritage and transport, the two cornerstones of the EU city agenda, were immediately placed front and center. It is worth noting that shortly afterwards Martínez Lapeña & Torres received the

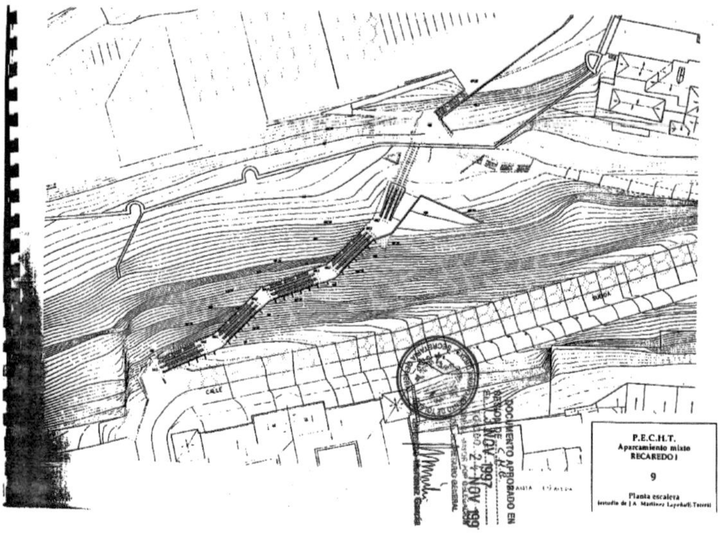

6 Plan of the fragmented Toledo escalators designed by Martinez Lopeña & Torres, 1997.
Source: Archivio Municipal de Toledo.

"Premio de Arquitectura Regional de la Junta de Castilla-La Mancha," which lauded the Toledo project for the same reasons. Even in the area of rewards, regional authorities tended to model their behavior on European patterns.

The EU prize assigns particular importance to the clients of the selected projects, who are always invited to the awards ceremony in Barcelona. The motto is a phrase attributed to Mies: "There is no good architecture without a good client." In the case of projects funded by the European Union, however, who is the actual client? When the *escalera mecánica* of Martínez Lapeña & Torres was selected for the European prize, the mayor of Toledo played the role of the client. Nevertheless, beneath the surface, there was another, hidden client, that not only paid for the project, but was also responsible for organizing the award.

The Project/Integrating Architecture

While the state has operated for centuries, ever since the time of Westphalia, as the central authority regulating architecture, European integration takes a different, more indirect approach. Given the mosaic of diverse interests and identities it represents, the EU cannot impose itself. Instead, it creates an economic incentive to develop projects that are in line with its agenda in terms of content and comply with its procedures in terms of method. Furthermore, at the other end of the process, it rewards those who play by these rules and excel at it.

In places like Spain, where the preeminence of the state was accompanied by a scarcity of resources, the arrival of European funds had a profound impact on architecture. On a fundamental level, it shifted the production of public works from the realm of the (top-down) plan to that of the (bottom-up) *project*. European integration unfolds through projects. It does not have a singular blueprint: instead, through its funding programs, it solicits, selects and shapes a plurality of projects, mostly originating at the local level.

Moreover, the projects that end up being funded are treated as *investments*. The term certainly has an economic connotation: the fact that the institution in charge of this process is a bank (the European Investment Bank) speaks volumes. However, it is also worth noting that European integration started as an economic venture, under the assumption that there can be unity and peace in Europe only as long as there is growth and stability. From this perspective, a project that helps the economy is also seen as an investment in European unity.

Unity, integration and cohesion, however, are pursued through a process that also generates fragmentation, decentralization and what Liesbet Hooghe and Gary Marks have described as a multilevel structure of power. Despite the rhetoric of a new Spanish architecture, EU funding is structured in such a way as to bypass national boundaries and empower local and regional authorities to interface with larger, common institutions. On the other hand, such realignment is made increasingly complex by the fact that the European Union is far from a monolithic entity and, instead, represents a balance of different forces. For example, while the European Commission operates on a supranational level, the European Council, which has authority over the European Investment Bank, responds to a different logic, moving forward through intergovernmental agreements. The result is a process that unfolds in a gradual, irregular way, often taking one step backward to take two steps forward.

The description of *La Granja Escalator* provided by the jury of the Mies award was, unintentionally, a perfect description of how European integration works. The citation applauded the "zigzag figure" designed by Martínez Lapeña & Torres, as it "prevented the sensation of vertigo that may be caused by a single tract staircase" (Fig. 6). It also appreciated its ability to engage with a difficult context "formed by the centuries-long accumulation of brushes," establishing a connection between the past and the future. While introducing a new "voluminous construction," the project had the merit of respecting the existing structure, to the point that the foundations of the escalators were built under the old foundations of the medieval walls. For the jury, this transformation was able to achieve "minimum visual impact," while becoming "the most characteristic element" of the city. Reading between the lines, the stairway of Toledo, in addition to being a product of European integration, comes across as a spontaneous metaphor of that process — the complex, fragmented stairway to Europe.

References

"About the Prize. Objectives", in *EU Mies Award*, www.miesarch.com/about-the-prize/.

Ayuntamiento de Toledo. *Pliego de Concurso para la Redacción del Proyecto de Remonte Mecánico y Aparcamiento en el Paseo de Recaredo*, November 13, 1997. Toledo: Archivo Municipal.

Ayuntamiento de Toledo, European Investment Bank. *Convenio entre el Ayuntamiento de Toledo y el Banco Europeo de Inversiones para el Proyecto de Renovación Urbana de Toledo*, July 23, 1997. Toledo: Archivo Municipal.

Baggio, Marianna et al., "The Evolution of Behaviourally Informed Policy-Making in the EU". *Journal of European Public Policy*, monographic issue *Behavioural Governance in the Policy Process*, XXVIII, 5, 2021, 658–676, and https://www.tandfonline.com/doi/full/10.1080/13501763.2021.1912145.

Barthes, Roland. *The Eiffel Tower and Other Mythologies*. New York: Hill and Wang, 1979.

Bergdoll, Barry. *European Architecture 1750–1890*. Oxford: Oxford University Press, 2000.

Busquets, Joan. *Toledo y su Futuro. El plan especial del casco histórico*. Toledo: Ayuntamiento de Toledo, 2000.

Bussière, Éric, Michel Dumoulin, and Émilie Willaert, eds. *The Bank of the European Union: The EIB, 1958–2008*. Luxembourg: European Investment Bank, 2008.

Clark, Greg, Tim Moonen, and Jake Nunley. *The EIB in the City: Investment on the Agenda*. Luxembourg: European Investment Bank, 2019.

Conde Bajén, Agustín. "Historia de una escalera." *ABC Toledo*, March 2, 2006, now in ABC, https://www.abc.es/espana/castilla-la-mancha/toledo/abci-historia-escalera-200603020300–142570195146_noticia.html.

"Escaleras de la Granja en Toledo. Martínez Lapeña — Torres arquitectos." *Arquitectura Coam*, 325, 2001, 40–45, now in COAM, https://www.coam.org/media/Default%20Files/fundacion/biblioteca/revista-arquitectura-100/2000–2008/docs/revista-articulos/revista-arquitectura-2001-n325-pag40–45.pdf

"EU Architecture Prize — Mies Award." *Fundació Mies van der Rohe Barcelona*, https://miesbcn.com/prize/.

European Investment Bank, *Annual Report 1997*, now in European Investment Bank, https://www.eib.org/attachments/general/reports/ar1997en.pdf.

Fabbrini, Sebastiano. "Against the Plan. The Architecture of European Integration." *Archimaera*, monographic issue *Rückseiten*, 9 (2021), 151–166, and https://www.archimaera.de/2021/rueckseiten/5218/archimaera9_fabbrini.pdf.

Fernández-Galiano, Luis. "Spain Disclosed." *Arquitectura Viva*, 104 (2005), 21.

Hein, Carola. *The Capital of Europe: Architecture and Urban Planning for the European Union*. Westport, CT: Praeger, 2004.

Hooghe, Liesbet, and Gary Marks. *Multi- Level Governance and European Integration*. Lanham: Rowman & Littlefield, 2001.

Koolhaas, Rem. *Elements of Architecture*. Köln: Taschen, 2018.

Koolhaas, Rem, et al., eds. *Harvard Design School Guide to Shopping*. Köln et al.: Taschen, 2001.

Magone, José M., ed. *Regional Institutions and Governance in the European Union*. Westport, CT: Praeger, 2003.

Majone, Giandomenico. *Dilemmas of European Integration: The Ambiguities and Pitfalls of Integration by Stealth*. Oxford: Oxford University Press, 2005.

Martínez Lapeña, José Antonio, Elías Torres Tur, *Memoria del Proyecto*, 22 December 1997. Toledo: Archivo Municipal.

McLean, Renwick. "Financial History Lessons for Europe's New Members." *The New York Times*, July 26, 2005, 6, and https://www.nytimes.com/2005/07/26/business/financial-history-lessons-for-europes-new-members.html.

Morata, Francesc. "Spain: Modernization through Integration," in Hanf, Kenneth, Ben Soetendorp, eds. *Adapting to European Integration: Small States and the European Union*. Harlow: Longman, 1998.

Patel, Kiran Klaus. *Project Europe: A History*. Cambridge: Cambridge University Press, 2020.
Piattoni, Simona, and Laura Polverari, eds. *Handbook on Cohesion Policy in the EU*. Cheltenham: Edward Elgar Publishing, 2016.
Riley, Terence, ed. *On-Site: New Architecture in Spain*. New York: Museum of Modern Art, 2006.
Ruiz Cabrero, Gabriel. *The Modern in Spain: Architecture after 1948*. Cambridge, MA: MIT Press, 2001.
Sorkin, Michael, ed. *Variations on a Theme Park: The New American City and the End of Public Space*. New York: Hill and Wang, 1992.

Chapter 7
Conclusion: European Governance and the Troubles of Building

Abstract

Due to its complex supranational dimension, the European Union occupies a unique position in the chessboard of global governance. Since the start of the integration process in the 1950s, the creation and expansion of the European institutions has led to the production of a substantial amount of architecture. Despite the power of these institutions, however, their buildings are largely unknown and, when put under the microscope, come across as wildly inadequate. Whereas national institutions rely heavily on architecture, embracing its ability to project power and shape political culture, supranational institutions operate in a different way. The representational tools that architecture brings to the table are viewed as a problem, something to be minimized or avoided as much as possible. Analyzing several significant case studies, one simple question keeps coming up: why is it so difficult for the European institutions to engage with architecture? This chapter focuses on this struggle and attempts to identify some its underlying causes, addressing the tension between the national and the supranational, the historical bond between architecture and the state, the shortage of acceptable images of Europe, the processual *modus operandi* and the functionalist culture of the European institutions, as well as the legal constraints that have limited their operations in the built environment. At the root of this impasse is a political deficit. For a multi-level union that has evolved around a model of depoliticized governance, institutional buildings represent a challenge, as they may bring about unmanageable political questions. The transfer of power to the European sphere comes with a neutralization of architecture.

Building the Supranational

The study of global governance and its architectural hardware tends to expose an asymmetric relation: the significance and complexity of the institution is rarely matched by the building that houses it. As pointed out by the editors of a recent issue of the *Architectural Theory Review*, the global organizations that emerged in the second half of the twentieth century mostly settled for objects of "little architectural interest."[1] While the initial expectation was that the institutions of the post-war liberal order would somehow produce their own architectural idiom, capable of expressing power in new ways, the results ranged from the aseptic to the banal, usually echoing the language of large corporations. Often, those who have approached these cases through the lens of architecture's traditional role, as a force that could represent ideas of power and shape political culture, have been left high and dry. But why is that? What are the reasons for such withdrawal?

This conclusive chapter considers a set of objects that speak to the aforementioned asymmetry in a rather extreme way: the institutions of the European Union. Paradoxically, although the architectural discourse has been plagued by a deep Eurocentrism, we have largely ignored this material, which relates to the most significant political and economic transformation in the old continent over the past seventy years. The process of European integration is worth exploring for two intertwined reasons: its unique supranational dimension and, largely because of that, its reluctance or inability to engage with architecture in any conventional sense.

As the term is often used, improperly, to describe institutions that operate at the international, transnational or multinational level, we shall first clarify what "supranational" means. In 1951, the Treaty of Paris marked the beginning of the integration process, establishing the European Coal and Steel Community — the first ancestor of the EU.[2] On that occasion, the foreign ministers of the six founding nations (France, West Germany, Italy, Belgium, Luxembourg and the Netherlands) signed a declaration, highlighting their "determination to create the first supranational institution and lay the true foundation of an organized Europe."[3] This was the first time the term "supranational" was used in an official capacity, as the legal concept chosen to characterize the method for the organization of the new community. At the heart of this project was the idea that power, in addition to being shared between (*inter*) nations, needed to be transferred, in certain areas, to an entity above (*supra*) them.

This entity is more than the sum of its parts, more than a space of cooperation and negotiation. A supranational body is supposed to have the autonomy, authority and legitimacy to make its own decisions and express its own will. Even though the member states keep playing an important role in the governance of the EU, mainly through the European Council and the other intergovernmental fora, the underlying logic of the integration process is to gradually separate power from statecraft. It is worth remembering that this process began in the aftermath of World War II, as eve-

1 Sven Sterken and Dennis Pohl, call for papers "The Architecture of Global Governance," *Architectural Theory Review* (2022).
2 Desmond Dinan (ed.), *Origins and Evolution of the European Union* (Oxford: Oxford University Press, 2006).
3 The joint statement of the six foreign ministers was issued at the signing of the Treaty of Paris, on 18 April 1951. It came to be known as the "Europe Declaration" or "Charter of the Community."

ryone had just witnessed the consequences of nationalism pushed to its limits. The space of the supranational, therefore, is not just a space where nations come together and pool some of their powers: it also entails a project of *nation-unbuilding*.

This tension, which has had reverberations into a multitude of spheres, is behind most of the reasons it has been so difficult to produce architecture for the European institutions. Nevertheless, since the 1950s, the advancement of the integration process has made necessary a large amount of architectural hardware.[4] The European Union now has seven decision-making institutions, spread over four cities, in dozens of buildings that house around 60,000 fonctionnaires, plus several other agencies and advisory bodies. While these are the control rooms of one of the largest democratic polities in the world, most EU citizens do not even know what this architecture looks like. In a recent survey, designed to test the efficacy of "European symbols," the buildings of the community institutions were not even included in the list of options.[5] The closest thing was Brussels, with its European quarter, which was perceived as a "good symbol" by less than 40 % of the interviewees.

Those who do recognize this architecture tend to regard it as wildly inappropriate or deficient as a representation of the European project. The former president of the European Parliament famously remarked that the building of his own institution in Brussels looked like a butt squeezed into compressing underwear.[6] For the locals, the building is commonly known as "*caprice des dieux*" due to its resemblance to the packaging of a popular French cheese. It would be kind of funny, if not for the fact that this is the seat of the biggest parliamentary assembly in the Western hemisphere, representing a population of 450 million.

This architecture-in-spanx is the result of a troubled history.[7] As it is now widely known, the building was developed in secret, because the French government opposed moving the institution away from its initial seat, in Strasbourg. For the entirety of the development process, the massive complex that came to house the European Parliament in Brussels was camouflaged as an "international congress centre." Then, once the building was completed, the national decision-makers were presented with the *fait accompli* and pushed to make a deal, in order to allow some of the parliamentary activities to take place in Brussels. The effort was promoted and funded by a group of private investors, led by two Belgian banks, which commissioned the design to a local, 26-year-old architect.

4 Carola Hein, *The Capital of Europe: Architecture and Urban Planning for the European Union* (Westport: Praeger, 2004).

5 François Foret and Noemi Trino, "Standing for Europe: Citizens' Perceptions of European Symbols as Evidence of a Banal Europeanism?" *Nations and Nationalism* (May 2022).

6 Comment made by Martin Schulz, who served as president of the European Parliament from 2012 to 2017. Rainer Wieland, the current vice-president for buildings of the European Parliament, discussed it at the conference *Architecture and the Institutions of the European Union*, held at Birkbeck, University of London in 2022.

7 Ludovic Lamant, *Bruxelles Chantiers: Une Critique Architecturale de l'Europe* (Montreal: Lux, 2018).

Recently, the department of politics at Birkbeck, University of London held a conference titled *Architecture and the Institutions of the European Union*. One by one, each building of the European institutions was given a close reading, in a dedicated panel, with contributions from architects involved in its design, functionaries who work in it, as well as political scientists and architectural historians. Although they had no background in architecture, the organizers of the conference were keen to explore what, if anything, these buildings "tell us" about the position and function of their institutions within European governance.[8] While the aforementioned case of the Parliament may seem extreme, the same type of stories kept coming up, revealing a deep rift between the ambitious vision of the "common European house" and the reality of the actual houses in which the community institutions operate.

Legal Constraints

Multiple issues have contributed to deepening this rift, making "supranational architecture" a very difficult proposition.[9] Let's begin with the most tangible issue, which concerns a legal restriction. For the first 42 years of the integration process, from 1951 to 1993, no formal decision was taken regarding the location of the European institutions, which therefore did not have the legal authority to directly produce and own their premises.[10] During this long period, they settled in Brussels, Strasbourg and Luxembourg, without an overarching plan, having to navigate the obstacles of their "provisional" status. The encumbrance to make a home for them fell on national or regional authorities, often in collaboration with private actors, which then rented the buildings to the European fonctionnaires.

The building of the European Commission, the supranational institution *par excellence*, is perhaps the clearest example.[11] First of all, it was set up in Brussels in the 1950s simply because Belgium preceded the other member states in alphabetical order: in the absence of a decision regarding its location, the initial idea was to rotate its seat between all the national capitals — a complex logistical challenge that was quickly let go.[12] In the end, the Commission never left Brussels. But, at the same time, its presence in the Belgian capital kept a provisional status for decades.

8 Dionyssis Dimitrakopoulos, introduction to the conference *Architecture and the Institutions of the European Union*, held at Birkbeck, University of London in 2022.
9 Sebastiano Fabbrini, "Whatever Happened to Supranational Architecture?" *Ardeth*, no. 7 (2020).
10 Koen Lenaerts and Kristien Vanvoorden, "The Legal Status of Brussels as European Capital" in *Brussels and Europe*, ed. Roel De Groof (Brussels: ASP, 2008).
11 Sven Sterken, "Bruxelles, Ville de Bureaux: Le Berlaymont et la Transformation du Quartier Léopold," *Journées du Patrimoine, Région de Bruxelles-Capitale*, no. 15–16 (2015).
12 Philippe Van Parijs, "Why did Brussels Become the Capital of Europe? Because Belgium Starts with Letter B," *The Brussels Times*, 7 September 2014.

The project for its headquarters, the Berlaymont building, was carried out during this time by the Belgian government, in collaboration with local real-estate developers. As it was unclear whether or not the Commission would remain in Brussels, the Berlaymont was initially designed to house a Belgian ministry: thc local authorities did not want to make a large investment for a European institution that might have left after a few months. The result was a building that never fit the modus operandi of the Commission, as evidenced by a long series of attempts to adapt and transform a space that was not conducive to a supranational operation. Suffice to say that the initial structure did not include appropriate facilities for translators.

As soon as the first group of fonctionnaires moved in, the interior layout of the Berlaymont had to be completely changed, to fit the various departments of the Commission, which required a high degree of autonomy from each other. This is how the maze of enclosed spaces, characterized by long dark corridors and offices without windows, came to be. It later turned out that the partitions used to reframe the space were full of asbestos, so the entire building had to be shut down and renovated. The Belgian government did not have the resources to pay for this renovation, so it brough in a group of investors—large financial institutions such as Citibank and BACOB, which took over the project in exchange for a long, advantageous lease on the building. They then sublet the Berlaymont to the Commission at a much higher price.

At every road bump, the European officials made the case for leaving a building that had been designed for something else and never really fit. However, the local authorities argued that, over the years, the Berlaymont had become a "symbol" of the European presence in Brussels and therefore needed to be preserved.[13] By the same token, when the Commission decided to create a logo in the mid-2000s, the choice fell on the silhouette of the Berlaymont. In the end, a building that had been shaped by national agendas and private speculations, required constant modification and threatened the health of its inhabitants, ended up representing the "visual identity" of the most important supranational institution.[14]

Against the Plan

This long period, more than four decades, of provisionality and powerlessness on architectural matters is the result of multiple tensions. Firstly, it was obviously difficult for the member states to agree on a permanent location for the community institutions, as any choice on a specific city would have favored a member and made others unhappy. It took until after the signing of the Maastricht Treaty of 1992, which reformed the community and established the European Union as we know it today, to

13 Chris Shore, *Building Europe: The Cultural Politics of European Integration* (London: Routledge, 2000).

14 European Commission, *Visual Identity Manual* (Brussels: European Commission, 2017).

make a final decision, which was essentially a formalization of the polycentric network of capital cities that had emerged, more or less spontaneously, in the previous years.[15]

But there was also another motivation. In the early 1950s, Jean Monnet, who is often described as the "architect" of the integration process, floated the idea of, one day, grouping all the European institutions in a single place, a federal district on the model of Washington DC.[16] The institutions never acted on this proposal but, at the same time, what came to known as the "Monnet doctrine" contributed to preventing, for decades, the recognition of Brussels, Luxembourg and Strasbourg as permanent seats of power.

Nevertheless, Monnet's idea inspired multiple actors, outside the institutions, to elaborate more or less utopian plans for the said European federal district, especially in the early phase of the integration process. Unlike the Berlaymont, these efforts were very much informed by the ambition to produce a representation of European unity, focusing heavily on the symbolic. Perhaps the most utopian plan was the one drafted by American planner James Marshall Miller, who proposed to build a capital city on the shores of a new artificial lake, created at the juncture of Germany, France and Luxembourg—a lake that was to be supplied by the water of all the major European rivers.[17] Miller went as far as to build an altar on the chosen site, which was to become not only the center of the city but also a sanctuary for European integration.

Along with other similar proposals, such as those for Wissembourg and Saarbrücken, Miller's "Lake Europa" never came close to being considered by the European institutions. Most of the proposals for a European Washington DC relied on the idea of creating a supranational district on the border between France and Germany. This meant that both nations had to cede a piece of land, which, in the aftermath of World War II, was easier said than done. But there was also a deeper, methodological problem. These proposals had two features that clashed with the very logic of European integration. In all these cases, the designers put forward grand, comprehensive plans and set out to deliver a symbolic representation of what European unity, in its highest aspirations, could look like.

As made clear by Robert Schuman in his famous declaration of 1950, European integration was not going to operate through grand plans.[18] While there are multiple different interpretations and definitions of European integration, everyone agrees on one thing: it is a process.[19] It proceeds gradually, exploiting spillovers and favorable contingencies, often taking a step back in order to take two steps forward. As a result, it could

15 Carola Hein, "The Polycentric and Opportunistic Capital of Europe," *Brussels Studies*, no. 2 (2006).

16 Jean Monnet, *Memoires* (Paris: Fayard, 1976).

17 James Marshall Miller, *Lake Europa: A New Capital for a United Europe* (New York: Books International, 1963).

18 Kiran Klaus Patel, *Project Europe: A History* (Cambridge: Cambridge University Press, 2022).

19 Antje Winters and Thomas Diez, eds. *European Integration Theory* (Oxord: Oxford University Press, 2004).

never be a goal-oriented endeavor. Political scientists refer to this as the issue of "finality." In an influential speech, Joschka Fischer described the unification of Europe as a "gradual process with no blueprint for the final state," that is a process without a plan.[20]

This was not an accident, but rather a design decision, which must be understood in the context of the *milieu* from which the European project sprang forth. Philip Almendinger, Anthony Fontenot and others have talked about the "growth in anti-planning thinking" in the post-war period.[21] In Europe, plans were being reassessed as instruments of control and domination, associated with modern statehood and, most importantly, its nationalist degenerations. A clear example can be found in the work of Friedrich August Hayek, who drew a direct connection between grand plans and totalitarian regimes.[22] European integration was set up in a different way, as to avoid the risk of making those mistakes again. Hence, when presented with a comprehensive plan for a European capital in a place like Saarbrücken, which had already been subjected to multiple invasive, transformative plans during German and French occupations, the European institutions did not even want to touch it.[23]

On the contrary, in Brussels, a city that has always been allergic to planning, the European institutions found the ideal soil to take root, as they gradually occupied office space without an overarching vision, embracing the "failing-forward" method.[24] Philippe Van Parijs has described the development of what is now known as Brussels's European quarter as a "snowball process" — a definition that aligns with the overall modus operandi of the community.[25] As the snowball was allowed to keep rolling freely for over four decades, a large amount of architectural hardware was produced and then rented to the European institutions by national or regional actors, in collaboration with private developers. On the other hand, all the bottom-up efforts to imagine a coherent space of power and give form to Monnet's vision remained on paper. It was very much a rift between unplanned buildings and unbuilt plans.

Hyperbolic Understatements

When this long phase of provisionality ended in 1993, as the heads of state and government of the EU finally decided regarding the location of the community institutions, how did things change? The practices that had been established, more or less infor-

20 Joschka Fischer, *From Confederacy to Federation: Thoughts on the Finality of European Integration*, speech delivered at the Humboldt University in Berlin, 12 May 2000.
21 Philip Allmendinger, *Planning in Postmodern Times* (London: Routledge, 2001); Anthony Fontenot, "Notes Towards a History of Non-Planning," *Places Journal* (2015).
22 Friedrich August Hayek, *The Road to Serfdom* (London: Routledge, 1944).
23 Sebastiano Fabbrini, "Against the Plan," *Archimaera*, no. 9 (2020).
24 Erik Jones, Daniel Kelemen and Sophie Meunier, "Failing Forward? Crises and Patterns of European Integration," *Journal of European Public Policy*, vol. 28, no. 10 (2021).
25 Philippe Van Parijs, cit.

mally, over the previous forty years had become very difficult to change. Path dependency matters. So, for example, many European institutions kept renting their buildings, well after they no longer needed to, because that had become the normal way of doing business.

But the most interesting element of continuity between the pre-Maastricht buildings and the post-Maastricht buildings concerns the understatement or the outright avoidance of any symbolic reference to the European project. That was to be expected in the case of objects produced by national actors or private speculators. However, after the European institutions acquired the power to drive their own architectural projects, such reluctance must be viewed in a different light.

The clearest example is the building of the European Central Bank, an institution that was established right after the signing of the Maastricht Treaty to oversee a reform that, by all accounts, constituted the most significant "deepening" of the European community since its inception: the creation of a common currency.[26] The area of monetary integration is certainly the one in which the process of supranationalization has gone the furthest. As noted by Howarth and Loedel, "it is the ECB that perhaps best defines the relinquishing of state sovereignty to an institution with powerful supranational mechanisms of decision-making and enforcement."[27]

As soon as the ECB was established, the heads of state and government decided that it was to have its permanent seat in Frankfurt. The new institution was therefore able to purchase a site from the city and signed an agreement with the German federal government, which underlined the independence of the bank and the "inviolability" of its premises. On this basis, the ECB launched an architectural competition, appointed a jury to evaluate the proposals and, overall, managed the entire process that led to the inauguration of its headquarters in 2015. Furthermore, it all happened during the debt crisis, when financial matters were the absolute priority, and the ECB became the *de facto* government of the European Union. Designing the ECB headquarters during those turbulent times was therefore a unique opportunity to help shape the institution that, more than any other, had come to effectively exert power in the complex space of the supranational.

From the competition brief onward, however, the ECB understated this opportunity and put the emphasis on issues of functionality. According to Kees Christiaanse, one of the renowned architects sitting in the jury, the ECB saw itself as a "service institution" and, therefore, was not looking for "great monumentality" or "extreme formal expression."[28] For example, the jury commended one of the proposals, which was awarded the third prize, because it "refrained from creating a unique and distinctive

26 Dorothee Heisenberg and Amy Richmond, "Supranational Institution-Building in the European Union," *Journal of European Public Policy*, vol. 9, no. 2 (2002).

27 David Howarth and Peter Loedel, *The European Central Bank: The New European Leviathan?* (New York: Palgrave, 2005).

28 Kees Christiaanse, interview by the author, October 2021.

landmark" but was "efficient, technically and economically feasible."[29] For Francis Gross, one of the executives who oversaw this endeavor from the inside and served as the secretary of the jury, the emphasis on the functional and technical aspects of the building, rather than its unique status as a supranational body, spoke to the "culture" of the ECB: "we can actually see that an institution's approach to architecture reflects its approach to its mission, which can raise some concern."[30]

At the same time, the architects who took part in the competition proved to be uninterested in or incapable of challenging said culture. The winning project by Coop Himmelb(l)au was a mix of high-tech envelope, which fit into the narrative of functionality and sustainability that the bank wanted to push forward, and a formal gesture that no one bothered to explain: "the design concept of the ECB is to vertically divide a monolithic block trough a hyperboloid cut, wedge it apart, twist it and fill the newly created intermediary space with a glass atrium."[31] Even though the architects presented it as a "unique, iconic building" that would become a "symbol for the European Union," it is not clear what the hyperboloid cut was supposed to say about the EU and the specificity of this institution. Ironically, six years later, a very similar design was submitted to the competition for the new headquarters of the Central Bank of Azerbaijan in Baku, which Coop Himmelb(l)au also won.

Blending In

Concurrently, a similar project was undertaken by another supranational institution, the European Court of Justice, which needed a major extension of its Luxembourg premises in the 2000s. In this case too, after a competition, the task was assigned to a high-profile architect, Dominic Perrault, who reorganized the complex and introduced two new "pencil-thin gold towers."[32] In spite of the size and impact of the extension, the institution constantly presented this effort in terms of functionality, efficiency, flexibility, cost-effectiveness, sustainability, security.

As noted by political scientist Sabine Saurugger, if one had to analyze the representational dimension of the project and extrapolate an image of the EU, the adjectives that would come to mind are "slick and elegant."[33] Again, the architectural output revolved around a refined but mute gesture, accompanied by a rhetoric of

29 European Central Bank, New ECB Premises—Minutes of the Jury Meeting—Second Phase of the Competition, 12–13 February 2004. ECB Archives.

30 Francis Gross, interview by the author, October 2021.

31 Coop Himmelb(l)au, *European Central Bank—Project Information*, 2014: http://www.coop-himmelblau.at/architecture/projects/the-new-premises-of-the-european-central-bank-ecb/.

32 Jonathan Glancey, "Let There Be Light," *The Guardian*, 2 December 2008.

33 Sabine Saurugger at the conference *Architecture and the Institutions of the European Union*, held at Birkbeck, University of London in 2022.

functionality. In a recent conversation with Joachim Schwiers, the director of the ECJ building, I asked what is unique about this space and how it distinguishes itself from the seats of national, regional or even private institutions. The answer was that the ECJ is on television more often.[34]

Unlike other institutions, especially state institutions, that have historically been quite deliberate in instrumentalizing architecture for representational purposes, the European institutions are very cautious in this regard. Partly because it is difficult to produce symbols when you have not fully defined who you are (the issue of identity) or where you want to go (the issue of finality).[35] But there is also the concern that, given the complex and fragile nature of a supranational democracy, any projection of power may be perceived as overbearing or, even worst, illegitimate and generate a nationalist backlash. As a result, when it comes to architecture, the goal is not to stand out, but to blend in.

In the case of the ECB headquarters, for example, it is not difficult to see continuity between Coop Himmelb(l)au's tower and those of other financial institutions based in Frankfurt, a couple of kilometers down the Main River, such as Commerzbank or Deutsche Bank. Interestingly, the European institutions seem to share the anxiety that, for completely different reasons, informed the approach of several post-war German institutions, including Frankfurt's Bundesbank. Wolfgang Voigt has pointed out that, after the traumatic experience of the Nazi regime, when it came to designing new German institutions after the war, "any notion of the architecture being used as a statement of power was avoided at all costs."[36] For the European institutions, operating in stealth-mode is regarded as the best way to avoid frictions with national bodies, which would struggle to accept an overt representation of their loss of power.[37]

The tension between the national and the supranational heats up whenever the latter tries to put forward an image of itself. In the case of the ECB competition, for example, a third of the 71 proposals was rejected because, according to the jury, failed to "convey an appropriate image."[38] This issue is easier to navigate in the intergovernmental institutions of the European Union, meaning the bodies designed for negotiations between the leaders of the member states. For example, around the same time as the buildings of the ECB and ECJ, the European Council was also given a new home in

34 Joachim Schwiers at the conference *Architecture and the Institutions of the European Union*, held at Birkbeck, University of London in 2022.

35 Paolo Patelli and Bendikt Stoll, "Whose Europe? On the Construction of Symbols, Architectural and Immaterial, and the Post-National Condition," ed. Sophie Lovell, *Archifutures: Thresholds* (Barcelona: Dpr, 2017).

36 Wolfgang Voigt at the symposium *Unloved Modernism*, held at the Deutsche Bundesbank in 2015.

37 Giandomenico Majone, *Dilemmas of European Integration: The Ambiguities and Pitfalls of Integration by Stealth* (Oxford: Oxford University Press, 2005).

38 European Central Bank, New ECB Premises—Minutes of the Jury Meeting—First Phase of the Competition, 28–29 August 2003. ECB Archives.

Brussels. This institution does not respond to supranational logic: it provides a forum where heads of state and government, as well as national ministers, can meet and make deals. Conceptually, it may actually be closer to the United Nations than to most other European institutions. As a result, the institution's image can be easily found using the language of the mosaic or the patchwork.

In the new headquarters of the European Council, known as the Europa Building, the issue of symbolism was solved by composing a façade with a multitude of different windows, that were brought in from all European nations. For architect Philippe Samyn, this was meant to be a "philosophical statement" about unity in diversity—the official motto of the EU.[39] In this framework, the image of Europe can be generated through an assembly of national images. When we move into the terrain of the supranational, which requires a rescaling and redefinition (not simply a juxtaposition) of its national components, this approach is not going to cut it.

Nation Neutral

The first systematic attempt to think about a supranational architectural image unfolded in the area where, as previously noted, the process of European integration pushed furthest: the area of monetary integration. In the mid-1990s, a few years before the competition for its headquarters, the European Central Bank undertook the difficult task of developing a set of images for the new Euro banknotes. From the very beginning, the primary concern was "national bias."[40] As it was immediately clear that the notes could not feature human representations, the bank decided to embrace architecture.[41] However, the obvious option of putting forward images of iconic buildings or monuments, such as the Parthenon or the Eiffel Tower, was off the table. As noted by the committee that drove this process, none of these monuments was linked with the "idea of Europe."[42] In fact, it is almost impossible to find a monument that was not conceived according to or retroactively steeped in some kind of nationalist narrative. The alternative solution was to focus on "architectural styles," looking to "convey, without specific reference to any given building, a clear message on the architectural richness and unity of Europe."

39 Philippe Samyn, *New Headquarters of the Council of the EU—Project Description*, 2016: https://samynandpartners.com/portfolio/europa-new-headquarters-of-the-council-of-the-european-union/.

40 European Monetary Institute, Design Brief for the Design of a Series of Euro Banknotes, 1996. ECB Archives.

41 Sebastiano Fabbrini, "Architecting the Euro," *Architectural Histories*, vol. 9, no. 1 (2021).

42 Theme Selection Advisory Group, Interim Report to the European Monetary Institute's Working Group on Printing and Issuing a European Banknote on the Selection of a Theme for the European Banknote Series, 1995. ECB Archives.

While the instinct was to lean on Europe's historical heritage, the past presented itself as a minefield, a history of conflict, mostly colored by the dynamics of the state. In preparation for the Euro design competition, which was launched in 1996, the ECB put together an advisory group, tasked with producing a *sui-generis* survey of European architecture.[43] The goal was to select more or less 100 architectural images that could serve as a reference for the competition participants. First, this material had to be sanitized, excluding all the buildings that could be perceived as too nationally biased or politically incorrect. Then, the designers were specifically instructed not to reproduce these objects but rather use them as possible starting points for operations of stylization. The task was to turn a history of specific buildings into a history of generic styles.

The competition was won by Robert Kalina, the banknote designer of the Austrian National Bank, who understood the importance of this transformation better than anybody else. Rather than engaging with buildings, he elected to focus on what he called "architectural elements"—windows, bridges and gateways.[44] This elemental approach was meant to isolate architecture from its historical and geographical bonds, which would have undermined the supranational ambition of the project. Nevertheless, as soon as Kalina's designs were presented to the public, every single detail started to be questioned, looking for the slightest case of national bias. In particular, the editor of the British magazine *Bridge Design and Engineering* was able to point out a number of similarities between Kalina's bridges and actual bridges.[45] The BBC organized a show about it, giving this bridge expert a prime-time platform to illustrate how some of the images on the new banknotes seemed to be copied from well-known bridges, such as the Rialto in Venice or the Pont de Neuilly in Paris.

Under public pressure, the European Central Bank had to ask Kalina to modify his designs to make them less recognizable and more generic. Even though Kalina had taken full advantage of the first versions of Photoshop and other graphic software, aiming to distort his images and make them as "nation neutral" as possible, apparently it was not enough.[46] It turns out that it is not so easy to avoid national bias and, at the same time, hang on to a historical narrative that inevitably intersects with national dynamics.

43 Feature Selection Advisory Group, Selection of Design Features: Report of the Feature Selection Advisory Group to the European Monetary Institute's Working Group on Printing and Issuing a European Banknote, 1995. ECB Archives.

44 European Central Bank, *Euro Banknote Design Exhibition—Catalogue* (Frankfurt: European Central Bank, 2003).

45 Russ Swan, *The Euro*, 2010. Blog available at http://russswan.com/about/the-euro/.

46 Robin Stam, *The Bridges of Europe*, 2011. Tumblr available at https://thebridgesofeurope.tumblr.com/.

The case of the Euro banknotes speaks to the difficulty of dislodging both architecture and history from the web of the nation-state. Even the idea of relying on stylization failed to recognize that this practice had itself been historically rooted in nation-building efforts throughout most of Europe. Since the early nineteenth century, architectural styles had been primarily conceived as tools for the creation of national representations. As noted by Barry Bergdoll, this was the period in which "issues of style became matters of state."[47] But the bond is even deeper. The construction of architectural styles was part of a much larger project, driven by a new approach towards history. Patrick Geary pointed out that "the modern study of history was conceived and developed in the nineteenth century as an instrument of European nationalism."[48] Eric Hobsbawm put it more directly: "historians are to nationalism what poppy-growers are to heroin-addicts."[49]

The modern practice and theory of architecture was largely shaped by these forces.[50] Over centuries, architecture contributed to the definition of state power and, at the same time, was profoundly impacted by its development. On a practical level, statehood brought about the institutionalization of architecture as a discipline and a profession. To this day, in most European countries, the only way to become an architect is to graduate from a state-approved program and pass what is known as a "state exam." Then, in order to actually practice architecture, one has to become a member of a state-controlled professional organization, which in many nations is significantly called "order."

Behind this effort to institutionalize and order architecture was the recognition that it could be a key contributor to a political project that was, in essence, a spatial project. The Westphalian order was based on the principles of sovereignty and territoriality, which refer to the organization and control of a delimited space by a single authority.[51] Architecture was important not only because of its ability to represent that authority, but also because it could provide some of the tools to outline and implement a theory of power that was, more than anything else, a theory of space. Louis Marin's influential essay on Versailles traces this bidirectional relation in a particularly clear way, showing how the prince built the palace, and, at the same time, the palace (architecture) built the prince (the state).[52]

47 Barry Bergdoll, *European Architecture, 1750–1890* (Oxford: Oxford University Press, 2001).
48 Patrick Geary, *The Myth of Nations: The Medieval Origins of Europe* (Princeton: Princeton University Press, 2002).
49 Eric Hobsbawm, "Ethnicity and Nationalism in Europe Today," *Anthropology Today*, vol. 8, no. 1 (1992).
50 Lawrence Vale, *Architecture, Power and National Identity* (London: Routledge, 2008).
51 James Caporaso, "Changes in the Westphalian Order: Territory, Public Authority and Sovereignty," *International Studies Review*, vol. 2, no. 2 (2000).
52 Louis Marin, "Classical, Baroque: Versailles, or the Architecture of the Prince," *Yale French Studies*, no. 80 (1991).

The Political Deficit

This is the framework in which, to quote Manfredo Tafuri, "architecture undertook the task of rendering its work political."[53] The issue of the political is key. The common assumption is that architecture is inherently political.[54] A more precise assessment may be that architecture produces political effects. At a minimum, buildings are vulnerable to being turned into sites of political engagement, even when their makers and users have no intention of doing so or actively try to avoid said engagement. Beyond the other dynamics discussed so far, this proclivity can perhaps help explain, on a deeper level, why most organizations born of the post-war process of "liberal depoliticization" struggle to deal with architecture.[55]

Zygmunt Bauman has described this process as a gradual separation of power from politics.[56] The European project responds to this logic and, in fact, represents one of the most advanced attempts to neutralize the political dimension. After World War II, in the *milieu* from which this project emerged, the political was very much understood in a Schmittian sense, as a fundamentally agonistic, conflictual dynamic, that led to what everyone had just experienced in a very real way: war.[57] As noted by Gian Giacomo Fusco, "the political was conceived in modern political thought as an original conflictual dimension presupposed by the state."[58] From this perspective, the state was regarded as a mechanism to control internal conflicts and amplify external conflicts. Robert Walker has characterized it as the "politics of inside versus outside."[59]

This was precisely the dynamic that European integration aimed to overcome.[60] The initial proposal to create a European Political Community, based on a political statute, was immediately shut down in the early 1950s and, from that moment onward, the integration process was centered on economic and juridical bonds — a common market and a common legal framework. Excluded from the supranational equation from the get-go, the political never really found its way back into the process, as evidenced by the failure to pass the EU constitutional treaty in the mid-2000s.

53 Manfredo Tafuri, *Architecture and Utopia* (Cambridge: MIT Press, 1979).
54 For a window into the discourse on the political within the field of architecture and beyond, see the proceedings of the AA symposium "How is Architecture Political?" (2014), with contributions from Chantal Mouffe, Pier Vittorio Aureli, Reinhold Martin, Ines Weizman and Sarah Whiting.
55 Paul Fawcett et al, eds. *Anti-Politics, Depoliticization and Governance* (Oxford: Oxford University Press, 2017).
56 Zygmunt Bauman, *State of Crisis* (New York: Wiley 2014).
57 Carl Schmitt, *The Concept of the Political* (New Brunswick: Rutgers University Press, 1976).
58 Gian Giacomo Fusco, "The Neutralisation of the Political: Carl Schmitt and the Depoliticisation of Europe," *Journal of Contemporary European Studies*, vol. 30, no. 2 (2022).
59 Robert Walker, *Inside/Outside: International Relations as Political Theory* (Cambridge: Cambridge University Press, 2011).
60 Ernst Haas, *The Uniting of Europe* (Stanford: Stanford University Press, 1958).

Overall, the European Union took form and evolved around a model of depoliticized governance.[61] The concept of governance is commonly used when approaching power as distinct from or exceeding the centralized authority of the state. What is not always recognized is that the transition from government to governance implies a redefinition and rescaling of traditional forms of political engagement. For most organizations that respond to the logic of global governance, politics is a hindrance or, plainly put, is not good for business. They do not want to be seen as all-round political actors but as technical bodies, focusing on specific tasks and making neutral decisions.

This is something to be kept in mind when analyzing the architecture of the said organizations. Even when architects do their best to avoid it, buildings tend to come across as political statements. In the case of the European institutions, making political statements is the last thing they want to do. Architecture, however, forces them to step into that arena.

The case of the ECB headquarters in Frankfurt is a fitting example. The competition was geared towards producing a functional architecture that, despite its size, would not convey any overt message about the EU. As noted by Hauke Horn, the result was a building that spoke the language of the corporate high-rise and did not say anything about the political dimension of the ECB.[62] The effort to avoid political can also be traced in the move away from the city centre: both in Frankfurt and in the other "capitals" of the EU, the community institutions have been located just outside the urban centre — the *polis*.

Despite all these precautions, as soon as the ribbon of the ECB building was cut, thousands of citizens assembled around this new landmark to protest the measures carried out by the European institutions during the financial crisis. They did not see the ECB as a neutral service-institution, making technical decisions: they saw it as a political agent. On the very day of its inauguration, the building was immediately turned into a site of political engagement by EU citizens. At the inauguration ceremony, the ECB president gave a speech that reflected this tension, arguing for the "need to reconcile the economics of integration with the politics of integration."[63] This acknowledgment of the political had been made unavoidable by the grounding of the institution in a specific location — a building around which people could gather and make their voices heard. The difficulty of engaging with architecture traces back to this ambiguity. For institutions that want nothing to do with the political or, as in the case of the EU, have been unable to define their political path, architecture is a minefield, as any building, even the most aseptic, is likely to bring about unwanted questions.

61 Gary Marks, Fritz Scharpf, Philippe Schmitter and Wolfgang Streeck, *Governance in the European Union* (London: Sage, 1996).

62 Hauke Horn, interview by the author, September 2021.

63 Mario Draghi, Speech at the Inauguration of the New ECB Premises, 18 March 2015. ECB Archives.

Index